The Study of Organizati

STUDENTS LIBRARY OF SOCIOLOGY

GENERAL EDITOR: ROY EMERSON
Professor of Sociology
University of East Anglia

The Study of Organizations

David Dunkerley
Department of Industrial Relations,
University College, Cardiff

LONDON AND BOSTON
ROUTLEDGE & KEGAN PAUL

First published 1972
by Routledge & Kegan Paul Ltd
Broadway House, 68-74 Carter Lane,
London EC4V 5EL and
9 Park Street,
Boston, Mass. 02108, U.S.A.

Printed in Great Britain by
Northumberland Press Ltd, Gateshead

ISBN 0 7100 7231 7 (c)
ISBN 0 7100 7232 5 (p)

Contents

CONTENTS

General editor's introduction

Today sociology is going through a phase of great expansion. Not only is there a widespread general interest in the subject, but there is a rapid growth in the numbers of new courses at universities, colleges of further education, and elsewhere. As a result there is an increasing number of potential readers of introductory textbooks. Some will be motivated by general interest; some will want to find out enough about the subject to see whether they would like to pursue a formal course in it; and others will already be following courses into which an element of sociology has been fused. One approach to these readers is by means of the comprehensive introductory volume giving a general coverage of the field of sociology; another is by means of a series of monographs each providing an introduction to a selected topic. Both these approaches have their advantages and disadvantages. The Library of Sociology adopts the second approach. It will cover a more extensive range of topics than could be dealt with in a single volume; while at the same time each volume will provide a thorough introductory treatment of any one topic. The reader who has little or no knowledge in the field will find within any particular book a foundation upon which to build, and to extend by means of the suggestions for further reading.

Anyone who has taught introductory sociology courses will know that two major problems present themselves. The first is to explain what is after all a very complicated subject in a way which is comprehensible to the beginning student. The second is to maintain the student's interest. Many people approach the study of sociology for the first time because they have an interest in the current problem of society and they believe that such a study will provide them with a relevant basis for the understanding of those problems. Of course all sociologists do believe that the study of their subject is relevant to such an understanding. It nevertheless is regrettably true that many introductions to the subject and in particular many introductory textbooks present their arguments in ways which must leave the reader to ask how all this is relevant to the social milieu in which he finds himself.

Individuals in our society participate in, or are confronted by, a great range of organizations large, small, formal, informal, and with many different organizational goals. There is sometimes a tendency to think only of industrial and commercial organizations as examples for analysis, but, as Dr Dunkerley points out, there are many other possibilities in the fields of medicine, the military, and religion. The aim of the present volume is to draw together the many theories and approaches which have been, and are being, used in the study of organizations and to present them in a clear statement as an introduction to the field. The extent to which these different approaches are appropriate for the study of the whole range of organizations, and the extent to which, in detail, the examples mentioned really are analytically comparable, must of course be demonstrated by research. But this book should

viii

encourage the reader to explore further the many empirical studies which have been carried on in this theoretically stimulating and practically important field.

A. R. EMERSON

1
The study of organizations

Introduction

The study of organizations has come to occupy a central place in the social sciences in the past few decades—so much so that there are now distinctive disciplines centred around such study. Today, most sociologists and a great many psychologists would claim at least some interest in the study of organizations. This, however, is not to say that the study of organizations is a new phenomenon in the social sciences, and in the discipline of sociology in particular. In fact, the study of organizations has a history almost as old as that of sociology itself. The 'founding fathers' of sociology such as Durkheim, Comte, and Spencer made clear their interest in organizations. These writers were concerned with delineating the stages of development of a society and distinguishing types of social organization appropriate to these stages.

The approach used by these early writers on organizations was soon discredited because it was quickly realized that this macroscopic level of analysis was incapable of increasing our understanding of the internal workings of the organization or of explaining the organization structure.

An understanding of the functioning and structure of

organizations has thus become the primary objective of the modern study of organizations. This objective is examined from a historical point of view, showing the significant advances made in the study of organizations. It is intended that this approach will give the reader an understanding, not only of these advances, but also of the kinds of problems which still exist in the study of organizations today.

The organizational society

Organizations today are an accepted fact of life. Individuals are surrounded by organizations from the day they are born to the day that they die. The term organization covers such institutions as hospitals, schools, factories, offices, the armed forces, and so on. In modern society it is impossible to escape from the influence of organizations of one type or another. It was an awareness of this influence that encouraged the early sociologists to develop their interest in organizations. As seen already, however, this interest differs from the interest of present-day sociologists. The difference between the two is not simply the difference between the levels of analysis—whether macro or micro—but also between an interest in the external political sphere of society and the internal political structure of the organizations.

The study of organizations, then, has developed mainly as a result of the proliferation of large-scale organizations in modern society. It must be asked why these large complex organizations came to be such a dominant feature of society. The simple answer to this question is that Western capitalism demanded the growth of large organizations. Early capitalism depended upon the factory system of production, a system which developed towards the

2

end of the eighteenth century. In parallel to the growth of the factory system was the technological revolution, which heralded the emergence of steam power upon which the factory system came to depend. The combination of steam and factory brought together under the same roof workers engaged in different stages of production. These were distinctive features of this system of production—the grouping together of larger numbers of workers than there had previously ever been; a strict division of labour; and the demand for an occupationally and geographically mobile labour force. With all these features present, the factory system expanded, calling for a greater division of labour between tasks, more specialized tasks, greater co-ordination, specialist financial controls, and so on (Miller and Form, 1964).

This early industrial era passed on to what Miller and Form call the 'mature industrial era'. This era has variously been known as that characterized by urban society, mass society, or more simply, modern society. The type of organization to be found in the mature industrial era is that known as the bureaucracy. In sociology, as seen later, the word bureaucracy is used in a value-free sense and has none of the pejorative connotations that it possesses in everyday language. It merely describes a particular kind of organizational apparatus. The bureaucracy developed in modern society as a response to the growing specialized division of labour and the sheer size of organizations, not only in the industrial sphere, but also in the educational, 'social', political, and economic spheres.

Modern organizations have also become more bureaucratized because of factors such as formalization, decentralization, and rationalization. Formalization means the growth of the administrative work of the organization as the size of the organization increases. Accompanying

3

this is a need for records to be kept, for work schedules to be maintained, and so on. All this calls for a large administrative apparatus for which the bureaucracy is ideally suited. The term decentralization refers to the need in modern organizations for decision-making. More specifically, it refers to the authority given by the organization to individuals to take decisions which will have an effect upon the organization. Because of the increasing size of organizations, the authority to make decisions is delegated throughout the organization. Whereas in the factory system of production most decisions were taken by the head of the organization, the organization in the mature industrial system delegates decision-making throughout the organizational hierarchy. This delegation of the authority for decision-making facilitates the development of a strict hierarchy of control in the organization and also emphasizes the specialized division of labour. Both of these can be taken as features of a bureaucratic organization.

The third feature mentioned as contributing to the increasing bureaucratization of modern organizations in the mature industrial era was rationalization. The term rationalization is used here in the sense that economists use it, that is, as a process whereby mergers take place between industries so that the major company increases in size and the smaller company declines in importance, or one whereby organizations or units of the same company merge. A process such as this has been a feature of the British economic scene since the turn of the century, and still continues. Rationalization of organizations has also occurred in other sectors besides the industrial one. Hospitals, schools, local government have all experienced an increase in the size of their units owing to the 'takeover' of the smaller units. Increasing size, as a result of rationali-

4

zation, provides ideal conditions for the development of a bureaucratic organization.

To put the nature of these organizational changes into perspective a few figures concerning the size of organizations can be quoted. Aaronovitch maintained that the forty largest companies in Britain in 1950 earned around one-third of all the profits made in this country. The aspect of rationalization is demonstrated in the figures he quotes for 'takeovers'. Out of the hundred largest companies in Britain in 1954, one had been taken over by 1957, and eight more by 1961 (Aaronovitch, 1955). Another way of looking at this is to point out that 'the total assets of I.B.M. exceed those of Belgium or that General Motors could afford, in strictly financial terms, to buy out Argentina' (*New Society*, 18 September 1969). A comprehensive analysis of the size of organizations is presented by Florence (1964) who points out that, despite the rather alarming figures quoted above, the majority of British industrial organizations have remained small, mainly as a result of the nature of the technology and production process.

Early studies of organizations

So far we have discussed some of the more important reasons for the growth in the size of organizations. Also, it has been mentioned that the early sociologists responded to the challenge thrown up by the changes taking place in society. The most significant of these responses can be examined and discussed in more detail.

Karl Marx Marx is usually regarded as a sociologist with respect to his writings on the sociology of knowledge, his theory of social change, and his analysis of class conflict and alienation (Bottomore and Rubel, 1956). His writings on organizations are not usually recognized as being among his more significant analyses. However, lack of recognition should not decry the importance of his writings in this area of study. It has been pointed out that an understanding of the Marxist position on organizations and bureaucracy helps considerably in understanding the controversies that existed in this area at an early stage (Mouzelis, 1967).

Briefly, Marx's analysis of bureaucracy and organizations owes its source to a critique of Hegel's analysis of the state. Essentially, Marx accepts the Hegelian approach whereby the organization is the means by which the civil society (constituting the particular interests) and the state (constituting the general interest) come together. Marx's acceptance of this position is only at a very general level, for in accepting the structure, he radically alters the meaning that Hegel intended. Marx, in line with his propositions about class elsewhere, maintains that the state does not represent the general interest, but, rather, the interest of the ruling class. That is, the state represents a particular interest and this particular interest is itself a part of the civil society. The result of this situation, as Mouzelis points out, is that the bureaucracy becomes one of the tools of the ruling class and in doing so dominates the other social classes. As such, the bureaucracy is a particular social grouping although it is not a social class. Marx goes further than this by stating that the bureaucracy contributes nothing to society in the sense that an industrial organization does, but has a distinctly parasitic nature. In a class society, the bureaucracy is essential for maintaining the class barriers that exist, and as classes become more distinct, the bureaucracy becomes more and more indispensable.

Marx maintained that with the decline of class society, the bureaucracy would disappear—it would wither away in the same way that he claimed that the state would

6

wither away. Where there is no class and there are no class divisions, the bureaucracy no longer has any useful functions, it becomes redundant.

Although this is a very oversimplified analysis of the Marxist position, it is clear that Marx in his writings was deeply concerned with the effect of the large-scale organization upon the wider society with which he was concerned. His analysis, in pointing out the relationship between the bureaucracy and the economic and political spheres of society, provides a clearer understanding of the nature and the functions of the bureaucracy in modern society.

Robert Michels   Michels's research on the history of socialist and trade union organizations in Europe at the turn of the century gave rise to his now famous 'iron law of oligarchy'. Michels maintained that this law was 'the fundamental sociological law of political parties' and could be summarized by the statement, 'who says organization says oligarchy'. The 'law' can be applied to various types of organization despite the rather narrow interpretation Michels laid upon it by applying it mainly to political organizations of one kind or another.

Michels was concerned with finding a connection between the development of oligarchies in organizations and the basic characteristics of these organizations. Michels's argument can be summarized in the following way. Whenever a social grouping exists, there is need for a leader to emerge for that grouping. When the social group is a small one, the leadership of the group can afford to be weak and informal. In the case of the small social group, the leader emerges from the group by a spontaneous and natural process. Since the group is a small one, the leader can remain an integral part of the group; he can still participate in the activities which other members of the group

7

are engaged in and can share any decisions which have to be made with other members as well. The authority given to the leader by the group is strictly limited and, to a certain extent, this authority is of a temporary nature.

Many groups do not retain their small identity for ever and often increase in size. When this occurs, the leader of the group has a more positive function because of the greater number of functions the group as a whole has to perform. Michels, therefore, at this stage, establishes a basic relationship, that as the size of a social grouping increases then so does the size of the leader's authority, his personal power, and the amount of delegation permitted in the decision-making process. This is not to say that at this stage the leader is divorced from the rank-and-file membership of the group or the organization.

According to Michels, oligarchy arises in the group because only those members of the group who are given leadership positions are able to carry out the specialized and technical requirements of the job. As the size of the group increases, these requirements become more and more specialized and technical, and consequently, the ordinary member of the group becomes more and more separated from them. On the other hand, the leader of the group advances to a position where he has a greater monopoly of the techniques and requirements and as such he becomes indispensable to the group. Once the leader is in a position of indispensability his power over the other members of the group increases.

One result of this is that the leader is in a position to select senior assistants. Only the leader has the technical expertise and knowledge to select suitable candidates for senior posts in the organization. In this sense, senior posts become part of the personal prerogative of the leader. His position is even more consolidated by this procedure and it becomes even more difficult to oust him from his position since he is surrounded by individuals with a personal loyalty to him. As well as increasing his power, the leader also becomes increasingly independent of the lower-level members of the group.

From a psychological point of view, the ordinary member of the group or organization accepts the position whereby the leader increases his power, authority, independence, and indispensability. He accepts this because he is pleased to have someone else carry out the administrative tasks. He recognizes that he does not possess the expertise of the leadership and willingly allows the position to develop.

The two main factors discussed—the monopoly of expertise of the leadership and the willing submission of the ordinary members—lead to a kind of self-fulfilling prophecy (Merton, 1949). Michels maintains that leaders hold on to power because of a psychological drive towards power and authority. This proposition, however, has doubtful validity. Rather, the leaders are concerned with maintaining their position because of the status they possess apart from the other members of the organization. They become used to the attributes associated with this particular status—for example, their standard and way of living. Again, the leadership may regard its position as being for the benefit of the organization and of the members of the organization.

Given an oligarchic situation, there are several consequences for the organization. The most important of these is that the leadership, in its position of independence from the ordinary membership, may use its power for its own aims. Since a rift exists between the leadership and the rest, the policies for the organization which are decided upon by the leaders may not be in the interests either of the members or of the organization. If personal objectives are held by the leadership then a displacement of objectives can easily arise. The objectives pursued tend to be conservative in nature since this ensures stability in the organization, and the activities of the leader are thus not exposed to the membership.

The differentiation between the leadership and the rank-and-file membership, Michels maintained, is a universal phenomenon. In other words, oligarchy exists in all organizations. However, there are degrees of oligarchy so that there is not invariably a conflict of interests between the two groups.

Michels's findings have been substantiated elsewhere. For example, Berle and Means's (1933) study of a large industrial organization demonstrated that the ordinary shareholder, by only owning a small proportion of the total stock, was separated from the leadership of the corporation. The management of the corporation wielded the power of the organization and, as with Michels's political parties, became indispensable and self-perpetuating.

Michels's study was important not only for the derivation of the iron law. He also provides guides as to the functioning of organizations. Organizational characteristics such as the delegation of authority, the nature of power and conflict, the formation of pressure groups, and so on are discussed as derivatives of the main thesis and provide a major contribution to the sociology of organizations.

F. W. Taylor and scientific management The work of Taylor and other scientific managers such as Gantt and Gilbreth represents a change in the approach adopted to increase our understanding of modern organizations. Whereas earlier writers had been pure theorists, Taylor attempted to put his ideas into practice. The work of the scientific managers represents one of the first systematic

10

attempts in organizational action, albeit within the confined area of the industrial organization. It should be made clear that these men were not social scientists in the sense that we understand the meaning of the word today, they were simply industrial managers putting their ideas of the relationship between the worker and the organization into practice.

The basic idea of the scientific managers was to increase efficiency in industrial organizations. In the first decade of this century, when these ideas were first proposed, they were taken to be quite revolutionary in the sense that the aim of increasing efficiency in industry was a completely new one. Taylor and his associates saw that the cause of inefficiency in industry lay with the management, as it failed to control the tasks of the workers and also failed to pay the shop-floor workers an income which would satisfy them. In the past, according to Taylor, the workers had been left by management to work out their own procedures and schedules, and this had been so much the worse for the workers themselves, for management, and for the organization. Taylor's aim was to find ways of measuring the jobs of workers and ways to control the work flow.

The influence of the scientific managers has been a lasting one. Taylor succeeded in his aim of improving efficiency by various 'scientific' measures and, with refinements, these are still used today. Time and motion study is probably the most well-known technique, but payments by results systems and production control systems are as much a legacy of Taylor and his associates.

In many respects the ideas of Taylor were remarkably naïve, although it is easy to say this with the benefit of hindsight. He thought that if the industrial organization increased its profits, then, by a simple relationship, the wages of the worker would rise in the same proportion.

Given such a relationship, he considered it a simple step to convince the worker that ultimately the methods of scientific management were for his own benefit, viz. scientific management would lead to increased efficiency in the firm, increased efficiency would lead to increased profits, increased profits would lead to increased wages for the worker. Conflict in the industrial sphere, according to Taylor, would disappear because the worker would realize that he would be harming the efficiency of the firm and hence reducing the size of his wage packet.

Taylor and his scientific management colleagues have often been accused of 'dehumanizing' the worker and of treating the individual as a piece of machinery. This criticism, however, is not entirely fair to the scientific managers. They stressed that the right 'atmosphere' ought to obtain for their methods to be successful. The problem was that the right atmosphere was never attained and it appeared that the individual was being subjected to methods more suited to a piece of machinery. Quite simply, the reason for the methods never working out as they were designed to was that the scientific managers did not have a sufficient grasp of elementary psychology and sociology to motivate the individual in the 'required' direction.

The human relations school

The influence of Taylor and the scientific managers on the industrial work-group aroused much criticism and opposition. The idea that men could be made more and more efficient in the sense that a machine could, produced an inevitable reaction. This reaction consisted of bringing 'humans' back into the factory. Industrial psychologists and physiologists researched the problems associated with equating men with machines, and this research often took

12

the form of investigating fatigue and monotony. The methods used to make the factory more 'human' involved numerous environmental conditions such as heating, lighting, rest-breaks, the hours of work, and even the colour of the walls.

The Hawthorne experiments   The research carried out by Elton Mayo and his associates at the Western Electric Company in Chicago between 1927 and 1932 has become known as the Hawthorne Studies (the research site was the Hawthorne Works). The results of this research are well known and well documented (Roethlisberger and Dickson, 1961; Homans, 1951; Landsberger, 1958). The early Hawthorne Studies concerned a work-group of women in the relay assembly test room. The hypothesis was that output by the work-group could be related to the hours of work and to the number of rest-breaks. This hypothesis was not substantiated, but the investigators found it necessary to account for social factors in their research.

A further stage in the research concerned the now famous bank wiring observation room. The work-group in this room was studied for a period of six months and patterns of informal relations and interaction became evident. These patterns were uniform to the work-group as a whole but were inconsistent in relation to the objectives of the formal organization structure. Two distinct cliques were observed within the group as a whole—most of the workers belonged to one or another of these groups and there were very few 'isolates'. A certain degree of conflict existed between the two cliques, but despite this the whole group was united by certain social links which led to the development of common norms and to the enforcement of such norms. The norms of the group applied to behaviour known as 'rate-busting' (exceeding the informally set production norm), 'squealing' (informing on the work-group to management), and so on, and non-acceptance of these norms by group members led to sanctions varying from 'binging' (a form of punishment involving striking the arm of the deviant group member) to ostracism. There was also a norm dictating what was to be considered as a 'fair day's work'. There were several purposes for these norms and for the backing of the norms with sanctions in the case of violation.

The existence of the norms meant that the workers could have a greater control over their environment and consequently be less dependent upon management. They felt they were in need of environmental control because of the enigmatic position they found themselves in—not knowing whether increased productivity would lead to a reduction in piece-rates; having no guaranteed wage-rates. Another reason for the existence of such norms was to increase the security of their jobs because increased productivity could have led to redundancies since the study was conducted at the peak of the Depression. A third reason for the norms, particularly those affecting output, was to maintain group solidarity and hence reduce group conflict and dissensus.

The Hawthorne Studies have been one of the most discussed pieces of research in industrial sociology for several reasons. They showed that empirical research has an important role to play in the growth of our knowledge about organizations. They also made a significant contribution in discrediting the principles of scientific management by 'discovering' the informal organization and the way in which the work-group can influence the individual.

The Hawthorne Studies have led to further research on human relations in industrial organizations, despite the

14

fact that there have often been criticisms of the methods employed by the early investigators.

Further human relations research The role the supervisor played in the Hawthorne investigations was one of the reasons why further research was carried out. Social psychologists have concerned themselves with leadership styles in small groups. These leadership styles give rise to various social climates such as 'authoritarian', 'democratic', and *'laissez-faire'*. White and Lippitt (1953) and Lewin (1953) show that workers were most satisfied with their jobs under a democratic type of leadership. Subsequent experimental work related leadership styles to other social-psychological variables such as morale and participation.

Another result of the Hawthorne Studies has been to investigate the influence of the small group upon the organization as a whole. This approach has used the concept of interaction as the basic unit of analysis. The work of Homans (1951) has perhaps best exemplified this approach. He re-analysed the Hawthorne Studies using a conceptual framework of 'action', 'interaction', and 'sentiments'. The re-analysis was compared with other data on small-group studies and from this Homans has attempted to draw general conclusions about the small group.

The weaknesses of human relations The analysis of conflict in the industrial situation is the weakness most often cited by critics of the human relations approach (Sheppard, 1954 and 1949; Sorenson, 1951). The contribution of the approach in demonstrating that conflict can arise as a result of poor communications and ineffectual supervision has been significant. However, there has been no further analysis into the nature of conflict, for example, the nature of the conflict which arises because of a group's particular position in an organizational hierarchy. It is said that the human relations researchers have been too concerned with the nature of integration to examine the nature of conflict.

Other limitations of the approach arise from this neglect of conflict analysis. The role of trade unions, the analysis of strikes, and so on, were all largely ignored because of the general emphasis on integration, equilibrium, and harmony.

These and other weaknesses of the human relations approach (such as the weak methods of analysis) have really been overcome in more recent studies. Sayles's (1958) investigation into the behaviour of industrial work groups and Lupton's (1963) comparative study of two workshops demonstrate that the human relations school has by now achieved a greater degree of sophistication.

Summary

The aims of this chapter have been to introduce the concept of organization and to look at the important early attempts at analysing organizations. The term organization is taken to include industry, hospitals, schools, prisons, and the like, and from this their pervasiveness in our society is apparent.

Marx's analysis of organizations has been shown to be at the macro-level of analysis, explaining, in part, the relationship between organizations and society. Later writers have shifted their focus of analysis: Michels, for example, was concerned with the internal structuring of activities within organizations and the development of his 'iron law of oligarchy'. The human relations approach is viewed as a response to the writings of the 'scientific managers', but for both groups of theorists the emphasis is upon the individual within the organization rather than upon the organization as a whole.

2
The modern study of organizations

Max Weber and bureaucracy   The influence of Weber on many branches of sociology is still keenly felt today especially in his contribution towards making sociology more of a scientific discipline. His writings on the sociology of power, of religion, and on sociological theory in general are cited by many sociologists today as the authoritative works in their field. Weber's analysis of the structure and functioning of that type of organization which he defined as the bureaucracy has been no less influential. It is not possible to understand his analysis solely on the basis of his description and definition of the concepts involved. Weber himself was involved in so many aspects of sociological writing that his writings on bureaucracy can only be understood in relation to his adjacent writings. In the case of bureaucracy, a full analysis can only be achieved by briefly examining his general theory of power and domination.

Power, to Weber, had a special and distinct meaning. He defined it as 'the probability that one actor within a social relationship will be in a position to carry out his own will despite resistance, regardless of the basis on which this possibility lies' (Weber, 1957). For Weber, the concept of power could be distinguished from that of domination.

17

Domination involves the use of power, but can really be expressed as a special type of power relationship. This relationship is that in which the ruler feels and believes that he has the right to exercise power. By ruler in this context is meant the particular individual who is able to 'carry out his own will'. A further aspect of domination is that the individuals beneath the ruler—the ruled—feel and believe that it is their unquestioning duty to obey the wishes and the demands of the ruler. In a power relationship of this kind, therefore, both rulers and ruled legitimate the actions of one another. In some situations domination of one by another can be exercised in a conflict-free situation because of the legitimation of the actions of the rulers by the ruled.

Many situations of domination occur when a small number of individuals exercise power over a large number of individuals. When a situation such as this arises, there is need for some kind of organization to evolve, and with this organization there must inevitably be what Weber calls an administrative class associated with it. This administrative class is responsible for carrying out the orders and the instructions of the rulers at the highest level and, furthermore, it is responsible for acting as a communication link between the rulers and the ruled.

So far in Weber's argument there is the feature of legitimation of the power relationship between the rulers and the ruled, and an acceptance that there has to be some kind of administrative class of individuals to carry out the wishes of the ruled and to enhance communications between the two groups. On the basis of the argument so far, Weber produced a typology of domination. The types of domination delimited are rarely found, in pure form, in the world of reality. The three types of domination are distinguished by three types of legitimation. Each corresponds to a particular administrative apparatus in which domination operates. These three types of domination he called charismatic, traditional, and legal-rational.

Of the three types of domination discussed here *charismatic* domination is the least important. Charisma is an unusual and exceptional quality that the individual possesses. In dictionary terms, charisma means 'gift of grace'. A leader who is able to dominate on the basis of charisma must possess some exceptional quality to have reached the position in which he is able to exercise domination. There needs to be a continual reassertion of the leader's capabilities so that domination is legitimated on the basis of these works. If the charismatic leader can be regarded as a ruler, then the ruled have to have faith in the work of the leader. This explains why the leader has continually to prove his capabilities and capacities to the ruled. In a sense, with charismatic authority, the ruled can be equated with disciples in so far as they have faith in the person who is exercising power over them. It will be recalled that each type of power relationship or form of domination could be envisaged as having a special type of administrative apparatus pertaining to it and to it alone. For the charismatic type of domination it is often the case that there are not enough 'ruled' to warrant the existence of a special administrative machinery. However, where there is justification for one, the machinery tends to be very unstable and very loose. In cases where there has actually been a true charismatic leader, the posts in the administrative apparatus have usually been filled by the early converts and the really sincere believers. Their role has been that of acting as part of the communication link between the leader and the led.

The second of the three types of domination is that known as *traditional* domination. In this type of power relationship, the leader is able to exercise power because of the traditional rights and duties associated with his position. In effect, the traditional leader rules because of his ascribed status and his inherited status, rather than because of any achieved status. Of course, his status may increase if he is able to carry out actions which the ruled consider merit further status. There must be recognition and belief by the ruled that the way 'things' were done in the past was the correct way and the best way of doing them. In other words, the power that the ruler exercises is strictly defined by what has gone before. Thus, over time, customs and methods of working are established and these become part of the tradition of the administrative apparatus. The ruler has to operate within these parameters but, within them, his orders and the amount of information he passes on to the ruled are purely arbitrary and personal. The legitimation of this rule comes about because the ruled see the past and the traditional way of doing things as the 'best' way. Also, there is a large measure of personal loyalty towards the traditional leader exercising power.

The third type of domination is what Weber calls *legal-rational* authority. This type is by far the most important and the most pervasive. Basically the idea behind legal-rational authority is that individuals have a sense of right-ness about the way things are conducted within the framework of an established legal system. The law and procedures have been undergone to ensure that methods of working, degree of authority, and so on, are legitimated. Both sides of the power relationship have to agree that the procedure for working with specified methods has been followed in the correct manner, that is, that the procedure has been legitimated. The ruler himself is a product of this legal procedure. He has come to exercise power as a result of going through the correct procedures such as appointment by an objective assessor or election by the majority of the electors. The rules laid down for any action which might be taken by the legal-rational ruler are strictly defined, and the ruler must work solely within the confines of these rules. Any attempt by the leader to exercise power outside this area constitutes an illegitimate act and goes beyond the frame of reference laid down for that particular individual by the powers of the organization or group.

Whereas the other two types of domination had administrative organizations corresponding to them which were vague in nature and which at times need not necessarily exist at all, with legal-rational authority there is a strict type of administration. In sociological terms this is known as the bureaucracy. There is often confusion over the exact meaning of the term bureaucracy since in everyday language the concept has a pejorative connotation. In sociological terms, however, it has a well-defined meaning. More will be said about this below.

There are certain characteristics of the bureaucracy which Weber took to be universal. In the context of the general theory of power and domination, the characteristics can be understood in terms of a belief by both rulers and ruled that the rules and the legal order of the bureaucracy define in very strict terms what the procedures are for the bureaucrat. Also, the rules define the kinds of relationships that there ought to be between the bureaucrat and his colleagues, the bureaucrat and the public, and the bureaucrat and the ruler above him. In this kind of administrative situation, the ruler and the administrator come to power solely on the basis of the legal rules laid down and agreed upon by the whole organization. The rules of the bureaucracy itself are regarded as impersonal rules and these account for the kinds of relationships which the bureaucrat has with the various agencies listed above.

The rules provide more than an indication of the way in which relations are to be conducted. They also rationally lay down the hierarchy of the organization in terms of the number of levels of control, the authority of each position in the hierarchy, and the span of control of each individual in the organization. Again, these characteristics are dealt with in more detail below.

In the bureaucracy, the means of control are separated from the bureaucrat. Further, none of the component parts of the organization belong to the bureaucrat. Also, the means by which administration takes place do not belong to the bureaucrat. The rulers, to whom the bureaucrat is servile, possess the means of control, and only they, with the agreement of the ruled, can attempt to change the methods of working or policy control. There is nothing in the position of the bureaucrat that is capable of being appropriated by the bureaucrat himself. There is a strict division between the two aspects of the bureaucrat's life. There are both the private and the official aspects of his life which, under a legal-rational system of administration, are strictly separated. Under the other types of administration discussed so far there is not necessarily this separation. Thus, the traditional ruler mixes both his official and his private life (and income) in many circumstances. In one sense, then, this separation can be regarded as a defining characteristic of legal-rational forms of administration.

Other types of administrative arrangements can be delineated, and in fact were by Weber. However, these are rarely regarded as having any special significance for students of organization. One further type does warrant a certain amount of consideration—that is the collegial form of administration. The discussion of the types of administrative organizations taken into account so far has either implicitly or explicitly conveyed the idea that authority

22

is wielded on the basis of its legitimacy. Thus, with charismatic authority, the ruler rules by virtue of being inspired in some way or because he possesses some special gift—'the gift of grace'. Legitimacy in the case of traditional authority rests upon tradition. Despite the tautology of this statement, it has been shown that traditional authority rests upon the belief by the ruled in the 'rightness' of the past. The third type of authority, legal-rational, has legitimacy resting upon technical expertise which has concentrated itself at the apex of the organizational or administrative hierarchy. The ruler is accepted as such because of his recognized competence in the office which he holds.

Under the collegial form of administration, the authority of the ruler is legitimated because he himself is a professionally trained man. As such, the notion of a hierarchical structure as prevalent in the legal-rational type of authority may not exist. The professionally trained man may have authority over a peer simply because of his training. The professional is thus given a large degree of autonomy and independence over his peers and to some extent over his superiors. The school teacher or the university lecturer provide good examples of collegial forms of administration, which at the same time exist within the structure of a legal-rational form.

The point has already been made that in their pure form these types of authority are unlikely to exist in the real world. Inevitably, in the real world, there is a great deal of intermingling of these various types. An individual who possesses a degree of power will use various types of authority to exert his will over others. The typology of authority delimited by Weber is however a useful analytical technique in so far as it enables the student of organization to distinguish the different types of authority in the real-life situation.

This chapter deals with what we often call the modern organization. In these organizations—whether we call them modern, complex, formal, or whatever—the most universal type of authority is legal-rational in form. Other types are appropriate in certain circumstances, usually depending upon the degree of stability or change in the organization and its environment. The most appropriate way to describe the administrative apparatus corresponding to a legal-rational type of authority is to call it the bureaucracy. There is an assumption, therefore, that any organization which does not fully exhibit bureaucratic features of the nature in which Weber delimited them, is to be regarded as a departure from the 'best' type of organization. This would be an unjust way of examining organizations, for in reality when an organization departs from the bureaucratic model of Weber, it is often exhibiting features of one or other of the types of administrative organizations discussed above.

Weber's model of bureaucracy   Weber's description of the modern bureaucracy was a direct descendant of his analysis of the types of authority. As already shown in the previous chapter, complex organizations of the type Weber described were not new in our society. However, the modern organization differed from previous organizations in several ways, and it was to these differences that Weber addressed himself. In distinguishing the main, essential characteristics of the modern complex organization, he was not the first social observer. The work of Saint-Simon, Comte and Durkheim was, in part, concerned with this kind of analysis before Weber. However, of all these early writers on sociology, Weber gave the most thorough and complete analysis.

For Weber, the modern organization differed from previous organizations because of the basis of authority that it employed and legitimated. The legal-rational type of authority provided the modern organization with an air of legality and rationality which previous organizations did not possess. Two features of the modern administrator —cosmopolitanism and expertise—distinguished him from his predecessors. His authority over others was based upon these features and upon the other defining characteristics of the modern organization which Weber outlined. These are:

1 A division of labour such that the total organizational objective can be split up into specific tasks and defined in a fairly precise manner.

2 The existence of a hierarchy of offices so that the division of labour of tasks in the organization is made more efficient. The administrative hierarchy ensures that each office is supervised by the one above it.

3 Organizational operations are governed by a system of abstract rules and procedures. These rules and procedures eliminate the necessity to issue instructions for each particular task in the organization.

4 The bureaucrat conducts his business in an impersonal manner. Impersonality applies as much to his dealings with clients as to the routine organizational business.

5 The bureaucrat is employed by the organization on the basis of his technical qualifications and expertise and the organization provides a career for the individual.

In addition to these five defining characteristics, the modern organization can be distinguished on the grounds that it is more efficient than other types of organization. Weber considered that the bureaucracy, from a technical point of view, could attain the highest degree of efficiency possible. This was because 'bureaucratisation above all else offers the optimum possibility for carrying through the principle of specialising administrative functions according to purely objective considerations' (Gerth and Mills, 1948, p. 215).

Essentially, we have now presented Weber's view of the bureaucracy. This model has been regarded as a functional model since it relates the characteristics of the structure to efficiency. However, under certain conditions, these same characteristics can be shown to have dysfunctional consequences and it is to these that we now turn. Before doing so, a word must be said about the methodological structure of Weber's model of bureaucracy. In sociological terms, the model is an ideal type. Many criticisms of Weber's analysis are invalid because of the non-recognition of this fact. Many criticisms assume that Weber's model is a working model, an empirical model, and as such should correspond to the situation as it is to be found in reality. However, Weber did not set out to present a model which could be equated with the world of reality, rather his objective was to identify the administrative components of a particular type of organization. An ideal type is difficult to define or even to describe at any general level. The easiest way is to follow Weber's example and to describe and define the ideal way by what it is not. Firstly, the ideal type is not meant to convey the idea that the construct is typical in any way. Secondly, the ideal type is not a logical class or a simple type. Thirdly, it is not an extreme type. Rather, the ideal type refers 'to the construction of certain elements of reality into a logically precise conception' (Gerth and Mills, 1948, p. 59). The organization theorist must be clear about this notion of an ideal type especially when applied to Weber's model of bureaucracy.

The functional model challenged

Whereas in Weber's model the defining characteristics of the bureaucracy were related to efficiency to produce a functional model, later writers have described a similar model where the defining characteristics can produce a dysfunctional model of organization. There have to be appropriate conditions for the characteristics to produce dysfunctional consequences.

Merton's model of organizational dysfunctioning (Merton, 1949) is a direct challenge to the functional model presented by Weber. His approach is based upon the concept of 'trained incapacity' as detailed by Veblen and that of 'occupational psychosis' developed by Dewey. By trained incapacity is meant that 'state of affairs in which one's abilities function as inadequacies or blindposts: action based upon training and skills which have been successfully applied in the past may result in inappropriate responses under changed conditions.' It is Merton's contention that Weber did not recognize that there are limits to which the organization can go in striving for efficiency and rationality. Reliability, efficiency, expertise, and precision all have their limits. If this is true for the organization as a whole, then it can be taken to be true for the individual bureaucrat. There is constant pressure on the individual in the organization to conform to the patterns of behaviour laid down in it. The individual must be reliable and consistent. Devotion and loyalty must be gained by the organization from the individual. All of these demands made by the organization upon the individual are designed to ensure a high degree of discipline within it.

Given this situation, Merton maintains that strong feelings are often engendered by the organization and the individuals composing it so that there is constant emphasis upon discipline. The argument continues that an over-emphasis on discipline and the strong emotions attached to it can lead to a transference of sentiments from the organization to the details of work in hand as laid down by the rules of the organization. These, instead of being a means, become an end in themselves so that the process known as displacement of goals comes into effect.

Goal displacement leads the individual in the organization to a situation where he is unable to adjust to the prescribed system of action, which in turn leads to a degree of formalism and ritualism. An over-concern with the rules of the organization can interfere with its objectives and this leads to the familiar notion of 'red-tape'. The result of this analysis as presented by Merton is that those characteristics which were originally designed to promote efficiency in the bureaucracy have led to inefficiency under certain conditions.

Each of the characteristics laid down by Weber as the defining features of the bureaucracy can now be examined to see how they can all lead to the organization being inefficient.

1 The division of labour   The total objectives of the organization can be so split up as to produce a situation where the individual in the organization no longer has any notion of what the ultimate goal of the organization actually is. The contribution of the individual can be made so minute that the organization can alienate the individual from his work and from the organization.

2 The hierarchy   It will be recalled that the hierarchy exists primarily in the bureaucracy to ensure that each lower office is controlled and directed by the office above it—that is, to ensure that activities in the organization are co-ordinated towards the achievement of the organiza-

28

tional goal(s). The implication of such a hierarchy is that all technical knowledge and expertise is concentrated at the top of this hierarchy. If the bureaucracy is taken to exist in stable conditions, then this situation will probably prevail. But organizations are in a constant state of change. The study of the electronics industry by Burns and Stalker (1961) highlights the fact that, as the bureaucracy is faced with change and with an unstable external environment, the concentration of expertise at the top of the hierarchy is unlikely to produce an efficient organization in terms of the achievement of its stated objectives. In effect, what occurs is that those individuals at the top of the hierarchy still demand undivided loyalty from those individuals lower in the hierarchy and in conditions of change this situation can have dysfunctional results. It is almost as if the originally legal-rational basis of authority is transformed into a traditional type of authority.

3 Abstract rules   The assumption in Weber's model of bureaucracy is that the rules exist to cover every possible situation which may arise. Every situation is to have prescribed procedures which minimize the taking of irrational decisions by the individual. Situations must inevitably arise, however, where the bureaucrat has to use his own discretion (Jacques, 1961) and when situations such as this do arise, the individual has either to follow the rule that is nearest to the present situation, or refer the problem to his superior, or use his own initiative. Whichever course of action the bureaucrat takes, the result can lead to inefficiency in the organization. If the nearest rule is taken, the client may become dissatisfied as his specific problem is not being dealt with. If the problem is referred to the bureaucrat's superior, the assumption of greater technical expertise at the higher level is made—in many cases an unwarranted assumption. If the bureaucrat exer-

cises his own initiative, he is condemned for this kind of behaviour by the bureaucracy as it is against the rules.

4 Impersonality The inefficiency arising under this heading is similar to that arising from the imposition of the abstract rules. In situations where the rules apply to the problem in hand the organization can remain efficient. However, where there is no direct rule, the usual course of action may be to apply that rule which appears most appropriate in that situation. This involves the subjective evaluation of the situation by the bureaucrat which belies the existence of a formalistic impersonality.

5 Career The Burns and Stalker study mentioned above points out that the provision of an organizational career pattern in the bureaucracy may lead to inefficiency because of the goal displacement effect already discussed. The incentives of a career system can have such an effect that the primary goals of the organization are lost in the pursuit of a higher grading in the organization.

In addition to the defining characteristics of the Weberian model of bureaucracy leading to inefficiency in the organization, these characteristics can also lead to a dysfunctioning of the organization in much the same way as Merton's model has demonstrated. Although the model may be dysfunctional in terms of the characteristics of the organization, these dysfunctions together with the positive functions of the organization can help the organization survive in a hostile environment.

The clearest statement of the way in which these dysfunctions can aid the functioning of the organization is given in a series of examples by Blau (1956). Three examples can be discussed which demonstrate social structures working differently from the ideal-type conception as laid down by Weber.

30

1 A study was carried out on the U.S. Navy at a base on an island which was isolated from other influences. The study showed the breakdown of the formal organization, with natural leaders emerging and the formal organization being replaced by an informal organization. The tasks of the personnel, whether they were day-to-day or long-run tasks, were carried out in a spirit of efficiency and enthusiasm. The new ethos contradicted the ethos which might have been expected under the conception of bureaucracy laid down by Weber.

2 The second study has already been mentioned. It concerns the telephone bank wiring room of the Western Electric Company. In the bank wiring room the work of different grades of personnel was interchanged, production levels (ceilings) were established by the men, they gambled (against the management instructions), and there were two distinct cliques each having their own level of production.

3 A third example by Blau concerned some Federal Law Enforcement Agency officers who were reluctant to reveal to their superior their inability to solve a problem for fear that their chances of promotion and their rating by the supervisor would be affected. An unofficial system was established in the agency such that the work in hand was completed satisfactorily despite the difficulties associated with the supervisor.

By now, it is possible to draw a few general conclusions from the analysis so far. The defining characteristics of the bureaucracy can lead, in certain circumstances, to both inefficiency and dysfunctioning, in much the same way as Merton's model has demonstrated. Although the characteristics of the organization can present a dysfunctional model, these dysfunctions can aid the organizations

31

to survive in a hostile environment.

Blau has suggested several conditions by which the organization can adjust when it is suffering from dysfunctioning in its parts:

1 *Employment security* For the members of an organization to assume responsibility for finding new ways of solving problems they must have employment security.

2 *Internalized standards of workmanship* Employees must feel free to exercise initiative, but they must also feel constrained by direct operating principles in doing so lest their spontaneous actions interfere with the attainment of organizational objectives.

3 *Cohesive work-groups* Integrative interaction in the work-group generally relieves disruptive anxieties and liaisons and often leads to new common practices that contribute to operating efficiency.

4 *Split in managerial authority* There is a basic conflict between the employers' interest in reducing cost and the employees' interest in increasing their income. This conflict is basic and cannot be talked out of existence by good labour-managerial relations. Its detrimental effects on operations can to some extent be avoided by splitting the managerial authority. Salaries and wages can be determined by an independent body in accordance with legal statistics and some other agreement and this will remove from the employees the need to protect their economic welfare against the management of their own organization.

5 *Evaluation on the basis of clearly specified results* Evaluation of performance, on the basis of clearly specified results which employees are expected to accomplish in their work, encourages ingenuity and simultaneously assures the standardization necessary for bureaucratic operation.

These five conditions together with one or two others characterize the 'new face' of bureaucracy. Once these are met, necessary adjustments occur quite spontaneously within the organization.

The 'natural system' theorists

Gouldner (1959) distinguished two different approaches to the modern study of organizations—the one he called the rational model of organization and the other the model of organization as a natural system. The first model can be equated with the discussion above on the bureaucratic model of organizations as distinguished by Weber. The emphasis here is on the formal structure of the organization and upon the processes of rational decision-making, the function of which is the achievement of the organizational objective.

An interest developed in the second model which Gouldner distinguished for several reasons. The bureaucratic (or rational) model of organization was regarded as ineffective because of its static nature and its emphasis upon the formal structure. This model, it was claimed, could not approximate to organizational reality. The writings of the human relations school provided data on the existence of informal groups in the organization and the influence these had upon the organization. However, this had not led to a new approach to the study of organizations.

The new approach—the natural system view—arose from the interest of sociologists in other areas of study in the concept of the system and the subsequent growth in system theory. The system approach has its emphasis upon the whole, within which there are a large number of inter-related parts which are also interdependent. The analysis of these parts involves 'the simultaneous variation of

33

mutually dependent variables' (Henderson, 1936, p.12). These parts of the organization are treated in such a way that they have their own needs and goals so that the existence of these goals leads to the treatment of the bureaucratic goals as only one set out of a number of such sets within the organization.

Several important questions arise from the system approach, such as:

a What are the strategic parts of the system?

b What is the nature of their dependency?

c What are the main processes in the system which link the parts together, and facilitate their adjustment to each other?

d What are the goals sought by systems?

The emphasis is upon spontaneity. Thus, the structure of the organization is seen to be in a state of spontaneous equilibrium. Changes which do occur in the organization are seen as being spontaneous adaptations in order for the organization to survive under changed environmental conditions.

Briefly, then, the difference between the two approaches is that the bureaucratic model is concerned with rationality whereas the natural system model emphasizes spontaneity. A later discussion will show that, in fact, neither approach is strictly accurate in its interpretation of organizational reality. One approach neglects the informal aspects of organizations and the other neglects the strictly rational aspects. Both models have been used to explain the one organization, as with the discussion of the Hawthorne Studies (Roethlisberger and Dickson, 1961) where a distinction was made between the 'logic of efficiency' and the 'logic of sentiment'. Management of organizations has been explained in terms of a 'rational model', while worker behaviour has been explained in terms of a 'natural system' model (cf. Lupton, 1963). What is required is an integration of the two models.

Two of the specifically system theorists can be examined to demonstrate the fundamental ideas involved in this school of thought. Parsons and Selznick are usually regarded as being the two most important writers in this area.

Talcott Parsons   Parsons has made a significant contribution to our understanding of complex organizations by viewing the organization as a social system and subsequently providing a sociological analysis of organizations. The concept of a social system is a difficult one to comprehend but, at the level of generality required for this study, the parts of a social system can be identified. Basically, these are three : an actor, a status, and a role.

The actor can be seen as a finite and discrete unit operating within the larger whole, the organizational system. The actor is composed of an aggregate of drives, motives, aspirations, abilities, and capacities. A status can be regarded as a particular position in a system constituting a division of labour. Associated with the status are expectations, as well as certain defined rights and duties which are derived from the objectives of the system. A role is the dynamic aspect of status, but equally so, it is the dynamic aspect of the actor, since both status and role bear down upon the actor, although in rather different ways.

The parts of a system need to be identified in a more restricted sense as a contribution to system functioning. The notion of role as described above means that only the actor's role in the organization can contribute to system functioning. The role cannot exist without the actor or the status structure. In an abstract analysis the concern

35

is only indirectly with the actor and the status. These system parts which contribute to system functioning have been identified by Homans (1962) and others as:

Activity in that someone has to do something for the system to produce something.

Interaction in that once activity is established there must be contact between one actor and other actors such that communication will take place.

Sentiment in that whatever is done can be linked to a cognition of the actor as well as to the more abstract concepts such as rules and norms which give rise to a kind of structure.

The main features of the concept of a system may be summarized as follows:

1 A system is composed of (a) elements which are (b) related to one another in a definable fashion, so that (c) it becomes possible to speak of the 'whole' as something different from the mere aggregation of the parts.

2 The components of the system comprise (a) parts—in the sense of 'things' which can be called a population; (b) a dynamic contact or other form of interrelationship between these parts; and (c) a structure which can be seen and said to influence, guide, or control the dynamics of the contacts between parts, even if temporarily.

3 There are clear differences in the complexity of the structural and organizational arrangements necessarily built into the system so that it can assume a state of 'wholeness'. These differences are usually described as differences of 'level of complexity', such differences applying to any or all of the parts, the contacts, or the structure.

To revert, then, Parsons views the organization as a social

system and to explain organizations he uses his more general and extensive social theory. In this social theory, or functional analysis, the basic unit of analysis is the individual actor, and as such, the basic social relationship is the unit act. The unit act contains four irreducible basic elements which are not derived from any other element. These are the actor, an end or goal to which action is directed, means by which the actor can manipulate the situation, and, fourthly, elements or conditions which are not open to control by the actor. It is recognized by most commentators on Parsons that the schema defining the unit act owes much to the influence of Weber and particularly to Weber's analysis of meaningful action.

For Parsons, then, the nature of social action is the necessary starting point. All social action is directed towards the attainment of goals. Parsons delineates three different aspects of this process, of which the third is a derivative of the other two. The two basic aspects of the action system of the individual are gratificational and orientational. Parsons calls these cathectic and cognitive respectively. In other words, human action displays both desires and ideas. The third aspect is derived in the following way : 'Cognitive mapping has alternatives of judgement or interpretation as to what objects are or what they "mean". There must be ordered selection among such alternatives. The term "evaluation" will be given to this process of ordered selection.' (Parsons, 1951, p.7). Hence the third aspect is evaluational.

Parsons's entrance into organizational analysis arises from his analysis of the four system problems which he delimits elsewhere. Two of these problems are related to the external environment of the system, and the other two relate to the internal environment. Adaptation and goal attainment constitute the former, integration and latency

37

(or pattern maintenance and tension management) the latter. Adaptation is a process whereby human and material resources come to terms with and manipulate the environment for the achievement of the organizational goals. Goal attainment involves the co-ordination of activities for the accomplishment of the organizations' goals. Since this is the question of finding suitable means for the given ends, decision-making comes within the problem as do the norms which regulate these.

The internal problem of integration is that of establishing and maintaining a level of solidarity within the system or organization so that it may function properly. Finally, there is the problem of latency or of pattern maintenance and tension management. The former deals with the problem of the compatibility of the participant's organizational role with his obligations outside the organization. A harmony must be created for the expectancies of each to coincide. Tension management refers to the processes which ensure that the motivational commitment of the individual is sufficient for the task set by the organization for him.

According to Parsons, organizations differ from other types of social systems because of their 'primacy of orientation to the attainment of a specific goal' (Parsons, 1956, p.63). According to Parsons the four major system problems delineated above can be equated with four different types of organization. These are organizations orientated to economic production and to political goals, integrative organizations and pattern-maintenance organizations. Economic and political organizations require little explanation but it should be pointed out (Parker *et al.*, 1967, ch. 7) that the term 'political organization' implies more than simply the means by which government becomes operationalized —the sense which is usually attributed to it. Thus, organizations which are concerned with political goals are also concerned with the 'allocation of power within society'.

Integrative and pattern-maintenance organizations require a degree of explanation. The former are concerned with conflict resolution and with the motivation of the participants of the organization. Organizations of this type would include political parties, legal organizations, and various types of social control organizations such as mental hospitals. The final type of organization—pattern-maintenance—is concerned mainly with cultural and educational objectives, such as schools and colleges, the church, and the family.

On the basis of the four problems which any social system has to solve, then, Parsons presents a typology of organization differentiated on the basis of the goals of these organizations. This approach to the study of organization is known as the comparative approach and will be discussed in more detail later.

Philip Selznick The theory of organization proposed by Selznick is usually regarded as being in the tradition of the natural system theorists and can be summarized in his own words by identifying the major ideas within his frame of reference:

(1) the concept of organizations as co-operative systems, adaptive social structures, made up of interacting individuals, sub-groups, and informal plus formal relationships; (2) structural-functional analysis, which relates variable aspects of organizations (such as goals) to stable needs and self-defensive mechanisms; (3) the concept of recalcitrance as a quality of the tools of social action, involving a break in the continuum of adjustment and defining an environment of constraint, commitment and tension (Selznick, 1948, pp. 34-5).

39

This frame of reference can now be examined in rather more detail. Organizations, in Selznick's view, can be analysed from two different angles. They can either be regarded as an economy or as adaptive social structures. Basically, Selznick accepts the proposition that formal organization is both rationally ordered and orientated towards the achievement of goals. By saying that an organization is an economy, Selznick means that there is a system of relationships which defines the availability of scarce resources. By viewing the organization as an economy, then, Selznick sees the organization as being manipulated in order to increase its efficiency.

Contained within the formal organization is an element which cannot be regarded as a part of the formal structure. This is the non-rational element, and as seen previously, this element is as important in the functioning of the organization as the purely rational aspect of organization. The existence of this non-rational aspect of organization clearly indicates that an analysis of the purely formal aspects of organization will not provide an adequate explanation of organizational functioning. As well as being an economy, therefore, the organization must also be regarded as a social system. By taking account of systems or structural-functional analysis the emphasis is upon those factors which 'relate contemporary and variable behaviour to a presumptively stable system of needs and mechanisms' (Selznick, 1948, p.27).

In a sense, structural-functional analysis takes account of the individual in the organization far more than Weber's analysis of formal organization did. In Weber's mode, it will be recalled, functions are allocated to organizational positions, and not to the individuals who fill those positions. Systems analysis recognizes that the individual can bring his own 'personality' into the organization and that the interests and the goals of the individual are not necessarily those of the organization in formal terms. Demands which are thus made upon the individual by the formal organization may be resisted by him in several ways.

Selznick recognizes these points in his analysis of organizations and realizes that the important criterion in systems analysis is the 'maintenance of the system'. Selznick suggests several 'imperatives' for the maintenance of the system. These asserted elements can be listed, and require little explanation:

1 The security of the organization as a whole in relation to social forces in its environment.

2 The stability of the lines of authority and communications.

3 The stability of informal relations within the organization.

4 The continuity of policy and of the sources of its determination.

5 A homogeneity of outlook with respect to the meaning and role of the organization.

From a consideration of these imperatives, Selznick arrives at his frame of reference as presented above. The principle on which this frame of reference rests is 'to select out those needs which cannot be fulfilled within approved avenues of expression and thus must have recourse to such adaptive mechanisms as ideology and to the manipulation of formal processes and structures in terms of informal goals' (Selznick, 1948, p.34).

Summary

This chapter discusses the work of Max Weber on organizations. His original typology of charismatic, traditional, and legal-rational domination is delineated, and the kinds of administrative apparatus corresponding to these types is analysed.

In modern society, Weber's model of the legal-rational bureaucracy is most appropriate. This is presented as an ideal type and defined by five principal characteristics. This model is seen as a functional one which under certain circumstances, such as those discussed by Merton, can be regarded as a dysfunctional one. The analysis describes how each of the defining Weberian characteristics can in turn lead to dysfunctioning and this is substantiated by empirical examples. Several conditions of adjustive development are suggested for an organization suffering from dysfunctioning of some of its parts.

Gouldner has observed two major schools of thought in modern organization theory. The first is the functional-rational approach of Weber, the second is the view of the natural system theorists as characterized by Parsons and Selznick. The emphasis in the latter approach is upon spontaneity rather than upon rationality.

Parsons's structural-functional analysis is discussed and the theoretical development of his typology of organizations is traced by analysing the four system problems which every social system has to solve. Selznick's examination of organizations as adaptive social structures or as economies is also discussed.

The discussion of the functional and the natural system views of organizations indicates several conclusions. Firstly, the formal organization of the kind analysed by Weber does have conflicting expectations and implications, particularly with regard to stability and change. The formal organization has conflicting implications, also, with regard to the fact that informal relationships do exist between individuals within organizations. Secondly, it has been shown that although individuals are assigned to formal positions within the organization, they do not necessarily react to those positions in strictly formal terms. In other words, individuals do bring their personalities with them into the organization. Finally, it has been shown that the goals of the organization cannot necessarily be equated with those of the individuals who, in part, make up the organization.

3
Social psychological
theories of organization

So far in our analysis of organizations, we have examined the two most important currents of thought, what Gouldner calls the 'rational' and the 'natural system' views of organization. There are other theories of organization which can be delimited, but which are not generally regarded as having such a prominent place in 'modern organization theory'. Although it is difficult to call it a separate theory of organization, one important current of thought about organizations has been presented by social psychologists. Their work is examined below and is considered separately from the previous theories because of the difficulty of 'pigeon-holing' them in the way in which Gouldner has done.

The most important writers concerned with this school of thought are Simon (1957), Barnard (1938), Cyert and March (1963), and March and Simon (1958). The studies of these writers indicate that the initial objective is the study of the individual, in the economist's sense of the word—as a rational man, capable of making any decisions, of solving any problems, since all alternatives are made available to him. This 'ideal man' is able to foresee the consequences of his action in decision-making, and further-

44

more he has a system of preferences so that he can decide on what will yield the optimum utility. From the point of view of pure analysis, theorizing in this way can be useful, but the body of knowledge which is derived from such analysis must be viewed with a degree of suspicion concerning reality since the principle of 'other things remaining equal' applies.

This view of organizations emphasizes the role of decision-making by the individual organization member. The rationale for this approach is that the study of organizations is partially the study of decision-making. This dynamic element is important because the idea of an organization is really that there is activity among a group of individuals and, furthermore, that this activity is both planned and co-ordinated. This element in itself is a major distinguishing characteristic of formal organization, which is not found in other social 'agglomerations' such as primary groups. It follows that if an organization is a structure of individuals participating in planned and co-ordinated activity, then this very activity is directed towards goal attainment. And if these goals are to be attained then decisions need to be made to achieve this end, which means that every organization member, in contributing to goal attainment, is both decision-maker and problem-solver.

Decision-making by an organization member is very different from decision-making by the ideal rational man. Simon maintains that decisions involve two kinds of elements—the factual and value elements. What this implies is that when any rational organization member is presented with a set of alternatives in a given situation, he will make the same decision as any other organization member (who is equally rational) in the same situation. In the setting of reality, however, the organization member is not presented with the factual and value elements—part of

45

his role is to search for these and to base his decisions upon them. Clearly, different organization members in their respective searches will 'uncover' different factual elements and will possess different value elements, and subsequently make different decisions.

From an examination of individual decision-making, the analysis is expanded to analyse the individual organization member participating in the organization—that is, to look at the relationships between the decision-maker and the organization. The assumption so far has been that the individual is already a part of the organization, but it is necessary to understand why he in fact joins the organization in the first place and, further, why he carries on participating in the organization.

March and Simon call this the 'decision to participate' and this notion stems basically from Barnard's 'inducement-contribution equilibrium'. This means that an individual comes to an agreement upon joining an organization whereby he receives 'inducements' in the form of money or kind, in exchange for 'contributions' made to the organization. The individual makes this agreement and continues to make it (that is, keeps participating) only as long as the contributions he makes to the organization are equal to or less than the inducements he receives.

Once the individual has decided to participate in the organization, he cannot be regarded as an autonomous and independent unit pursuing his own goals, satisfying his own needs, making his own decisions, and solving his own problems. The organization sets limits upon all of these activities so that with decision-making, for example, his activities are restricted by the organization such that there is a pattern deriving from the activities of all organization members. It is necessary, then, to examine how the organization restricts the individual in this way in order that there should be a consistent overall plan and co-ordination of activities.

Any individual participating in any organization is restricted to what role he can play in the organization by the particular functional specialism he has. This being the case, the organization has a demarcated division of labour between activities which immediately delineates the decisional area of the individual. The individual is given a task and is allowed discretion only in the area germane to that task. The structure of authority within an organization will also limit the individual's area of discretion. The classical view of an organization is to view it as a working hierarchy on organization chart lines. In such a view, authority and subsequently communication place further limits upon the individual. In Simon's view, these limiting factors determine some of the value and factual elements which contribute to a co-ordination of the individual's decisions with the decisions of other organization members, although not necessarily restricting initiative and responsibility.

The stage has been reached whereby it has been shown that the organization is viewed as 'a system of consciously co-ordinated activities' (Barnard, 1938, p.72) and that activity is co-ordinated in the pursuit of common goals. Decision-making is concerned with the implementation of goals and the processes of decision are the means for achievement of the organizations' goals whereas personal individual goals are considered as one of the resistances of the environment. A rational decision can be made when both value and factual elements are given. However, this says little about how goals are derived.

Simon attempts to demonstrate that organizational goals are refined and communicated by the hierarchy of organization levels that serve as processing points for decisions.

47

Thus, when organizational goals are given, the decision chosen at one level sets the goals for the executive level below. As these are processed in their descent through the organization they become more narrow and defined. Hence, means at one level become the goals of the next, so that there is a continuous means-ends relationship throughout the organization.

The analysis can be further widened by moving away from looking at the individual organization member as the decision-maker and instead focusing upon the organization as a whole making decisions. There are several problems in reorientating the analysis in this way and certain factors have to be taken into account in doing so. The analysis presented here relies heavily upon the work of Cyert and March (1963).

Cyert and March approach the problem of analysing decision-making in the organizational context by examining the decision-making process *in toto*. In order to do this, they analyse the most important decisions that are taken by any economic organization (the firm) and, from this, attempt to understand the various processes within the organization which lead up to these decisions, by building empirical models of the situation. 'Trust Investment Behaviour' and 'Price and Output Determination' are examples of 'important' decisions taken by the organization. The rationale for approaching the problem in this way is that the empirical models might build something of a bridge between economic theory (in relation to the firm) and organization theory.

A bridge-building exercise of this nature is obviously a sensible one; since the two sets of theory are so much at variance and yet combined in some way, they could produce a worthy contribution to the understanding of the firm and hence the organization. Apart from the problem of

48

rational and non-rational decision-making in the two approaches, there is also the problem of who actually makes the decision. In economic theory, it is the individual, the entrepreneur, who makes the decision; organization theory has the organization or the firm as the decision-maker. In other words, in the latter approach, decisions are organizational, not individual ones. Furthermore, the analysis is made more complicated since both the position of the market (external factor) and that of the organization structure (internal factor) influence the outcome of a decision.

Because of these significant problems which arise in examining the two approaches, Cyert and March attempt to raise the status of the 'behavioural theory of the firm' to a more realistic and empirically-derived level. Their approach in attempting to achieve this necessarily involves considering the organizational elements in the decision-making process.

Cyert and March argue that the decision-making process of an organization can be examined by a set of variable categories and a set of relational concepts. The relational concepts are in fact the main building blocks for their general theory. The variable categories, affect organizational goals, organizational expectations, and organizational choice but on the other hand, the four relational concepts provide a pattern for the decision-making process and hence provide the more significant contribution to the general framework. There are four relational concepts referring to the major areas of decision-making and these can be examined in turn.

Quasi-resolution of conflict   Cyert and March point to the 'obvious potential for internal goal conflict in a coalition of diverse individuals and groups' (p.115). Traditionally,

49

this process of dealing with goal conflict was dealt with in the form of inducements. If an individual was given sufficient inducements, it was maintained, he would conform to the goals of the organization. The proposition here is that organizations are composed of individuals with conflicting values and goals, but that the individuals form a kind of uneasy coincidence or coalition from which there are bound to be certain interests, objectives, or goals which are held in common agreement. This process of achieving common agreement is known as the organization goal.

Potential goal conflict is partially resolved by the structural characteristics of the organization. Any organization has a division of labour based upon functional specialization and the way in which tasks are divided and allocated among the organization members is usually strictly defined by the organization. This being the case, general organizational goals are themselves divided so that, for example, there may be an organizational goal of achieving the maximum profit, but this goal is allocated among the various functional specialists such that one may be concerned with maximizing the sales of a product, another with maximizing production, and so on. It is only when these 'departmentalized' goals are brought into a coalition that an organizational goal can be said to exist.

Often, the goals determining the organizational goal may be in conflict—in the above example, the situation may arise where the sales specialists have 'sold' (on paper) or received orders for more goods than the production specialists can produce. In this way, it is clear that conflict can never be completely resolved, nor are organizational goals ever static or eternal.

Uncertainty avoidance   In reality, all organizations exist in an environment of uncertainty. Uncertainties arise from

50

various sources such as the market, competitors, the supply of raw materials, and so on. These uncertainties cannot be predicted in the long term and so organizations have two courses of action open to them. Either they predict the uncertainties in the short run, or they avoid the uncertainties altogether. In fact, the short run may be so predictable that there is no uncertainty, so the two courses of action can become one. As well as avoiding the uncertainties the organization can, of course, attempt to stabilize the uncertainty elements in the environment through planning. The important point is that organizations try to avoid uncertainty by whatever means available.

Problemistic search So far, the analysis has concentrated upon goals and matters of uncertainty—these concepts are concerned with the kind of ends sought by the organization. But to achieve any 'end' in any context there must be means available. And it is the search process which acts as the means in this general theory. Cyert and March assume that this search process is motivated, simple-minded, and biased. Organizational searching is motivated in that a particular problem always stimulates the search. Since there is this particular problem in all cases, there is a problemistic search. The search is simple-minded because the rules 'reflect simple concepts of causality'. In other words, there are simple rules for this procedure which avoid involvement in ideal rationality. Finally, there is the search bias. This arises in adjusting hopes to expectations which has the effect of decreasing the amount of problem-solving time required.

Organizational learning Cyert and March believe that in the same way that decision-making can be regarded as an organizational phenomenon, so can adaptation. Organizations can be regarded as adaptive systems so that whenever problems arise which cannot be dealt with by standard work procedures, changes will occur within the organization to deal with this.

These four relational concepts are all important for designing the general theory of decision-making by the organization. According to Cyert and March the decision-making process can be seen to follow this pattern if an organization is analysed from the commencement of evaluation of performance in relation to a certain goal. When the organization has successfully completed the steps in this pattern and the ensuing performance is considered to be satisfactory, then the effectiveness of using these decision rules is confirmed and will be used again. This demonstrates uncertainty avoidance. On the other hand, if the performance is unsatisfactory then a better alternative will be sought. If this search for an alternative turns out to be satisfactory then the search rules are reinforced. If the search is unsatisfactory then the search rules are changed and it may be that either new rules or less ambitious goals will be learnt by the organization.

Communication theorists

A final, and as yet relatively insignificant, way in which organizations have been viewed is to see them as communications media. This means that the analysis must necessarily focus upon the internal structure. Instead of the organization being seen as a decision-making unit, it becomes a decision-making system. In the former, the internal structure is taken as given, since the analysis is concerned with the total or aggregate behaviour pertaining to decision-making. Analysis of the decision-making system involves focusing attention upon the centres of decision and the way in which communication channels interconnect these.

The way in which the concept of system is used in this context differs from that already seen above. 'System' is used more in the sense that management theorists use it than that in which it is used by sociologists. The management theorist has developed his ideas on systems through the growth of an interdisciplinary approach to organizational comprehension, using the basic ideas about systems which are to be found in engineering, biology, and sociology.

The main concepts for this model come from 'communication engineering' and cybernetics. The use of cybernetics has been considered valuable because it deals with the analysis, design, and functioning of systems. Hanika (1965) defines a system in this context as 'any entity, conceptual or physical, which consists of inter-related, interacting or interdependent parts [where] these parts may, in themselves, be systems' (p.6). A cybernetic system is regarded as self-fulfilling: information about the behaviour of the system is fed back into it and it adjusts its behaviour as a result of this new information. Every cybernetic system must have a detector (receiving information about the state of the goal which is to be controlled), a selector (taking decisions about which way the system should go, on the basis of information received from the detector), and an effector (executing the decisions of the selector).

In this way, a position of equilibrium, or a state of homeostasis, is maintained in the system. When a situation arises whereby there is incongruence between the desired and actual state in the system, the detector will realize this and will inform the selector. On the basis of this new information, the selector will make a decision and order the effector to carry this out. Equilibrium is then restored to the system.

Viewing organizations in this way implies that they are to some extent self-controlled. Therefore, they should be adaptive to change. A cybernetic system is not rigid, and can alter its internal structure. Since the model has feedback mechanisms, it is highly suited to problem-solving. Communications can be very easily analysed because the model represents a self-controlled system.

Jaques (1961) has noted that communication links may spontaneously be limited to the transmission of certain types of material only. For example, a supervisor may pass along only that type of 'screened' information which he feels his superior would like to hear from him. Or, he may be faced with the problem of reducing the amount of information he can pass along simply because there is too much to tell. To describe the communication structure of any organization in a systematic fashion, it is necessary to specify for each position in the structure which other positions are connected to it by a direct channel of communication. The total pattern of positions and communication links constitutes the communication structure of a group. Once this has been determined every member of it can be located and these various locations can be characterized in various ways. Of course, in the same way that the communication structure can be specified, so also can the power structure, by determining the power relations between each pair of positions in the group.

Summary

This chapter is concerned with the work of theorists who cannot be labelled as theorists of formal organizations or as natural system theorists. They have been called social psychologists here because of the level of analysis used —emphasizing the individual and relationships between individuals. The principle characteristic of such theorists is their concern with the decision-making and problem-solving processes, initially for the individual and later for the organization as a whole. The pure theory of writers such as March and Simon and the applied theory of the 'firm' as developed by Cyert and March are examined.

The chapter concludes with a brief examination of the role of communication studies and cybernetics in the study of organizations. This is one area where the potential for future development is very great, particularly with the possibility of simulated computer models of organizations.

4
Methods of organizational analysis

In previous chapters we have examined the principal theories of organization that are prevalent today. In the past two decades a trend towards increased empiricism in sociology has been discernible and, as a specific branch of sociology, the study of organizations has contributed to this trend. By attempting to make empirical use of the various theories of organization presented above, researchers have encountered difficulties in adapting the theories to the empirical practice. In examining both work and non-work organizations, several contemporary researchers have found it necessary to start their analysis of organizations in different ways from those of earlier researchers.

One major way in which this can be demonstrated is to point out that the problems of bureaucracy and of rationality and formality in organizations, which at one time completely dominated organizational analysis, have now been largely discarded. In their place a new and major area of organizational analysis has been emphasized—that of the comparative analysis of organizations. Smith points out (Parker *et al.*, 1967, p.72) that the move has been towards making a comparative analysis of the formal structure of organizations and that the inadequacies of the Weberian model have provided the impetus for this.

Comparative analysis

Sociology has always used the comparative method of analysis, but in the area of the study of organization this method is relatively recent. There has been little agreement about what the comparative method, in general terms, entails. Spencer used the term in the sense of describing, at an intra-societal level, the same phenomena in order to prove his laws of social evolution. Alternatively, Durkheim used the same concept to demonstrate correlations between social phenomena.

Today, when the comparative method is used in the study of organizations there is a more general level of agreement as to its usage and non-usage. Most organizational analysts agree with Blau's definition of the method as 'the systematic comparison of a fairly large number of organizations in order to establish relationships between their characteristics' (Blau, 1965, p.323). This definition corresponds very closely to the meaning attached to the concept by Udy (1965) and Perrow (1967).

The meaning of the concept 'comparative analysis' is quite specific. Thus to some extent all organizational analysis involves this method but, by giving the concept a quantitative aspect referring to specific organizational attributes, a specific meaning is attached to it.

Most researchers using the comparative method have pointed out the differences of this method from the case-study approach to organizations. The single case-study approach has been criticized by methodologists for the assumption that the general can be derived from the particular. This reductionism argument is a valid one; however, it must be pointed out that until comparatively recently organizational sociology was in a fairly embryonic state. Only recently (say, in the last twenty years) has there been an increased interest in organizations with the resultant research findings. Users of the case-study method have justified their position by pointing out that the sheer size of modern organizations is prohibitive if more than one or two organizations are to be studied. If this argument is correct, then how can the comparative method be operationalized? It will be recalled that it involves the systematic examination of particular organizational attributes. Many of these attributes are very easily measured, without the necessity of a full-scale investigation into each organization.

Blau (1965) has attributed the emphasis upon human relations studies and studies of small groups in organizations to the single case-study method which has been used in the past. With the development of the comparative method it is postulated that greater strides can be made towards the attainment of a more universally accepted theory of organization.

It is not considered necessary to examine explicitly in any detail the theoretical assumptions associated with this approach nor to develop the various dimensions of the approach. This can be done implicitly by examining some of the more important studies in this area. Four studies are discussed below and in all but one of them the analysis covers all types of organization, both work and non-work. It will be seen that all these studies are attempts at providing valid typologies of organizations. The effectiveness of these attempts can be ascertained by an understanding of the basic functions of a typology. Essentially, these are predictive, comparative, heuristic, and classificatory.

Parsons An earlier chapter has indicated the significance of Parsons's work for the study of organizations. It will be recalled that an organization can be regarded as a social system, but that it differs from other systems because of the 'primacy of orientation to the attainment of a specific goal'. Four types of organization are delineated by Parsons which correspond to the four system problems—economic, political, integrative, and pattern-maintenance organizations. As seen above (p. 39), integrative organizations concern themselves with conflict resolution and attempt to motivate organizational members. Political parties and legal institutions provide good examples of this. Pattern-maintenance organizations have cultural and educational objectives—for instance, schools, the church, the family, and so on.

Parsons thus provides a theoretical typology of organizations so that they are 'pigeon-holed' on the basis of their objectives in relation to the total social system. This analysis is not usually considered to be very significant because of its high level of generality and the difficulties involved in operationalization.

Blau and Scott A significant development in the comparative analysis of organizations has been made by Blau and Scott (1963). They propose a typology of formal organizations on the basis of the criterion 'who benefits?' Four types of organization are delimited and organizations are assigned to one type rather than to another by asking who is the prime beneficiary. The emphasis is upon the 'prime' beneficiary rather than upon any other since, to some extent, most participants in any organization benefit from participating. With respect to any formal organization four types of person are distinguished: the members or ordinary participants, the owners or managers, the clients, and members of society.

By using these four basic types of person, a typology

59

of organization based upon the 'who benefits?' criterion results:

Type of organization	Who benefits?
1 Mutual-benefit associations	The membership
2 Business concerns	The owners
3 Service organizations	The client group
4 Commonweal organizations	The members of society

Blau and Scott recognize that this typology is not exhaustive, but that if it is combined with other classificatory exercises a more refined typology might result.

A discussion of the central problems confronting each of these types of organization highlights the usefulness of the typology as a whole, especially in relation to its empirical validity. Thus, for mutual-benefit associations there is the problem of maintaining internal democracy; business concerns are confronted with the problem of maximization of efficiency in a competitive situation; service organizations have the problem of reconciling potential conflict between the professional service and the administrative procedures; finally, for commonweal organizations the central problem is to develop democratic procedures which can be publically controlled externally.

Etzioni In his comparative analysis of organizations, Etzioni (1961) also arrives at a typology of organizations. At first sight this typology appears to be more exhaustive than the Blau–Scott typology. Certainly, it is more complex if only because of the criteria used to classify organizations.

The basic variable used in the typology is that of compliance. Compliance is utilized to examine the power relationship between those who exercise power and those

60

upon whom power is exercised. In order fully to understand this power relationship Etzioni distinguishes three 'kinds of power', three 'kinds of involvement', and also the way in which power and involvement are associated in certain situations. Organizations are classified by examining the associations of power and involvement.

The three 'kinds of power' delimited are coercive, remunerative, and normative. According to Etzioni these three kinds can be associated with three types of involvement respectfully. These three types are alienative involvement, calculative involvement and moral involvement.

Having established that these three kinds of power and three kinds of involvement exist, Etzioni (1961, p.12) then distinguishes instances of 'congruence' and of 'incongruence' viz.:

Kinds of power	Kinds of involvement		
	Alienative	*Calculative*	*Moral*
Coercive	1	2	3
Remunerative	4	5	6
Normative	7	8	9

Compliance (that is, the relationship between power and involvement) is congruent in cases 1, 5, and 9. These types of compliance are found far more frequently than the other six types given. Classifying organizations on the basis of this typology of congruency gives rise to three major types of organization. Firstly, there are 'total' organizations which use coercive power and result in alienative involvement. Secondly, there are work organizations using remunerative power and generating calculative involvement. Thirdly, the compliance relationship of normative power and moral involvement can be observed in many types of normative organizations such as religious, educational, and social service organizations.

Pugh and Hickson   Whereas the other three studies of comparative analysis are applicable to all types of organizations, the Pugh-Hickson classification deriving from comparative analysis refers specifically to work organizations. The fact that previous classifications have been too ambitious provides part of the rationale for the Pugh-Hickson classification; in addition, previous classificatory exercises have been *a priori* classifications with little reference to empirical testing.

Pugh, Hickson, and Hinings (1969) present a taxonomy rather than a typology of work organizations. The rationale for this is that taxonomies are multidimensional structures and are derived empirically. Typologies, on the other hand, tend to be unidimensional and *a priori*.

Fifty-two work organizations in particular were systematically studied and five structural variables examined—specialization, standardization, formalization, centralization, and configuration. These variables were measured by specific scales and any variance which resulted was explained by four dimensions of structure of which three were used as the basis for the taxonomy. Thus, a taxonomy is derived which applies to organizational structures rather than to organizations *per se*. The three crucial dimensions were structuring of activities, concentration of authority, and line control of work flow.

In looking at these three dimensions and at their interrelationships, a clustering of organizations can be observed, which forms, in effect, the taxonomy. A classification of seven types of organization structures results: full bureaucracy, nascent full bureaucracy, workflow bureaucracy, nascent workflow bureaucracy, pre-workflow bureaucracy, personnel bureaucracy, and implicitly structured bureaucracy. The relationship existing with the three dimensions used as the basis for the taxonomy is as follows.

TYPE		Structuring of activities	Concentration of authority	Line control of workflow
1	Full	High	High	Low
2	Nascent full	Less High	Less high	Less low
3	Workflow	High	Low	Low
4	Nascent workflow	Less High	Less low	Less low
5	Pre-workflow	Considerably less high	Low	Low
6	Personnel	Low	High	High
7	Implicitly structured	Low	Low	High

Pugh *et al.* argue that their empirical taxonomy of organization structures has implications for the concept of bureaucracy itself. The important finding is that 'bureaucracy takes different forms in different settings' and that the unitary concept of bureaucracy is not an accurate descriptive tool of analysis.

Levels of analysis

There is an implicit problem running through the above section on the comparative analysis of organizations. This problem can be made explicit and it is possible to analyse the way in which empirical researchers into organizations have attempted to overcome it. Basically, the problem is knowing which level of analysis to use. Thus from an examination of the comparative studies of organization, it is clear that different writers have used different levels of analysis. Parsons, for example, is concerned mainly

63

with the cultural and institutional level whereas Pugh and Hickson concentrate upon the structural level.

It is usual to distinguish three major levels of analysis—role, structural, and organizational. It is impossible to say which of these three levels is the best or the most appropriate one to use, because the level employed by an individual researcher is dependent upon what information he wishes to gain from his study. Nevertheless, each of these three can be systematically examined and, in particular, it is possible to look at the way in which they have been used in empirical studies.

Role analysis   The level of analysis which focuses upon the individual role has proved to be a useful one and also one which has been widely used by both theorists and researchers. By focusing upon the role, the behaviour and the attitudes of organizational members can be examined in so far as both are related to the working of the organization.

The study of organizations must necessarily be a residual function of the analysis of specific organizational roles. Organizational characteristics can be understood by focusing upon the individual role, but this understanding comes about indirectly. Comparative analysis of organizations is possible using this level of analysis, albeit in a very restricted sense, by obtaining individual responses about a certain issue and then by aggregating these responses. This procedure can be carried out in several organizations, and some comparison can be made. There is a danger in this method of reductionism, about which more is said in a later chapter. Basically, reductionism can be avoided by an acknowledgment that the 'whole is greater than the sum of the parts'. That is, at each successive level in the organization there are certain characteristics which are not present in the level below. Despite the danger of reductionism, the level of role analysis can make some contribution to the comparative study of organizations.

Role analysis is also useful in studying organizations when the roles examined are those of the 'key informants'. That is, individuals who hold the key positions in an organization can be analysed and compared with other individuals in the same organizational position in another organization.

In analysing organizations, then, the level of role analysis is useful, but the reservations must be recognized. If information is used which is of a factual nature, then the reliability of the method increases. For example, when normative or attitudinal data about individuals is used, it is less easy to make a strict comparison between organizations. Another point is that a large proportion of the total population needs to be investigated for any results to be reliable.

Structural analysis The second major level of analysis involves the investigator in an examination of the properties of organizational groups and of specific structural characteristics of organizations.

The main groups in an organization are examined, and in looking at the group the researcher is concerned principally with the social relations in the group among the individuals of which it consists. This method has proved to be a very valuable one (for example, the Hawthorne Studies). Whereas in role analysis it is usually only possible to examine a sample of the total number of individuals, in structural analysis all the groups in the organization can be studied. This arises from a simple operational equation in that there must necessarily be fewer groups in an organization than there are individuals.

When the focus is upon the structural characteristics of the organization, it has been pointed out (Blau, 1965) that the total organization is assumed to be problematical. Thus, the characteristics which are specifically organizational are not focused upon and it is not felt necessary to explain them in any way.

Organizational analysis The last level is the one most commonly used in the comparative analysis of organizations. Here, the investigator examines the specific characteristics of the organization itself. The way in which these characteristics are related to one another is also examined, as is the process which produces them.

The main objective in using this form of analysis is to examine the features of an organization which lead to its existence as a functioning whole. The entire organization is used in this method, instead of the individual organization member or the work-group.

These three levels of analysis, almost by definition, give rise to different types of organization study. The first, role analysis, cannot adequately provide for a comparative analysis of organizations. However, at the case-study level this method is particularly useful. The structural level of analysis, again, is useful for case studies, but not particularly good for an adequate study of more than one organization. Clearly, with the third type, the organizational level, is admirably suited to the study of more than one organization. At this level, the environmental influences upon the organization can be examined, in a way in which the other two levels are incapable.

In the same sense, there are 'best' methods to use when employing these three major levels of analysis. Thus, for role analysis, the interview provides the maximum information; for structural analysis, systematic observation is the most relevant; and for the organizational level, the comparative method is the best.

Blau (1965) examines Weber's model of bureaucracy in the light of the comparative study of organizations, using the organizational level of analysis. He concludes that the organizational level of analysis can provide the most systematic account of the operations of a bureaucracy. Minute details of day-to-day operating procedures (to be found from role analysis) or the structure and process of the social groups in an organization (to be found from structural analysis) do not really provide the kind of data required. Data to be found from the organizational level is restricted but, as Blau points out, this is precisely the kind of information which is required.

Summary

The comparative method of analysis is discussed as a significant recent development in studies of organizations. It enables several types of different organizations to be studied and propositions and hypotheses to be derived which are universally applicable.

The important research carried out in this area is discussed. The organizational typologies of Parsons, Blau and Scott, and Etzioni are examined together with the empirically derived taxonomy of Pugh, Hickson, and Hinings.

The problem of which level of analysis to use—role, structural, or organizational—is next discussed. It is interesting to note that previous studies of organizations have adhered to either role or structural analysis. Thus, in general, role analysis has been used in studies on hospitals and schools, whereas structural analysis has predominated in the study of industrial organizations. The chapter concludes by pointing out that the organizational level of analysis has to be used if comparative analysis is to develop as an important alternative in organizational sociology.

5
The organization and
its environment

Up to this point it has been assumed that it is a relatively easy task to identify an organization and that the boundaries of the organization are quite clearly defined. Until fairly recently, writers on organizations also made this assumption and even went further. In many cases, the organization was viewed as a closed system, an entity on its own having, as it were, very little contact with any phenomena beyond its boundary. The organizational characteristics have been systematically examined by many writers, but they have been taken to be simply characteristics which are internal to the organization. No account, in many cases, has been taken of external characteristics which, although not strictly properties of the organization as formally defined, can and do have an influence upon the workings of the organization.

This myopic approach to organizational analysis is nowadays rarely used. Writers on organizations have realized that factors external to the organization can have a considerable influence upon the workings of the organization. One reason for this realization has been the trend towards greater empiricism in organizational analysis and the resultant comparative analysis of organizations. Another reason, and probably a more important one, is that the work of empirical researchers has shown the effect of external influences upon the organization.

Today, then, most organizational research takes into account the influence of external factors. In many cases the organization is defined in a very vague way, thus demonstrating that the boundary between the organization and external influences is not as clear-cut as was originally thought. When a boundary is drawn between the two aspects, it is usually drawn for the sake of convenience, rather than because of ignorance. Further, the organization is invariably viewed as an open system, rather than as a closed one. External influences are examined as rigorously as internal ones.

Much of the discussion in preceding chapters has indicated the importance of the influence of external conditions. For example, the stable rational model of bureaucracy has been shown to be unstable in conditions of change. Gouldner's study of a gypsum plant demonstrated that the external community ethos carried over into the plant, and in many respects determined both work and social roles. One of the factors cited for restriction of output by workers in the bank wiring room of the Hawthorne Studies was fear of redundancy if too much was produced. These, and many other examples, illustrate that external conditions have been shown to influence internal relationships in an organization and, further, that they can structurally influence the organization.

Empirical studies have not been the only ones to recognize the importance of external factors. From a theoretical point of view, seeing the organization as a goal-oriented system requires that the organization survive in the face of what is sometimes a hostile environment. That is, the organization has to come to terms with, and acknowledge, the existence of the external environment.

It is not true to say that the whole of the external environment affects the organization and its internal functioning. Only certain aspects of the environment can be tied to the functioning of the organization. Of these aspects, two can be delineated as being the most important. These are the influence of the existence of other organizations, with which the organization interacts to a greater or lesser extent, and the influence of the technology of the organization. The latter can be regarded as an external or environmental influence for the purposes of this analysis.

The influence of other organizations

It is a fact of organizational life that all organizations must at some time or another, and to a greater or lesser degree, interact with other organizations. Sometimes other organizations can constitute the most important influence upon the particular organization in question.

All organizations are governed by governmental organizations to some degree; industrial organizations are often dependent upon banking and financial organizations or upon competitors or customers, who often take the form of organizations rather than discrete individuals. Clearly, then, each organization interacts with at least one other organization, and in most cases there will be several organizations having an important influence.

When several organizations interact, the possibility of conflict between them is greatly increased, so much so that Scott (1964, p.520) has said that this conflict is inevitable. Blau and Scott also see the likelihood of conflict (1963, p.195) and point to a number of mechanisms which are used to accommodate this conflict. Briefly, these include secrecy, publicity, and the development of mutual-benefit associations.

In their examination of the goals of an organization and the relationship between these and the external environment, Thompson and McEwen (1958) see four types of relationship between one organization and another: competition, bargaining, co-optation, and coalition formation.

Several writers have made the proposition that an organization is more likely to achieve its goals if it is able to achieve a high level of separation from its environment. Thus, the greater the dependency, the less the effectiveness of the organization. Greater autonomy can be obtained in industrial organizations, for example, by setting up a group which, as it were, sits between the organization *per se* and the environment of the organization. Thus, the board of directors fulfils this function in an industrial organization, the board of governors or managers in a school, and so on. Bodies such as these act as a link between the organization and the higher level, the institutional level (Parsons, 1960).

Perfect autonomy is impossible for any organization to achieve. In one sense, an organization is merely a partial social system since it is necessarily dependent upon other partial social systems for the satisfaction of its needs. Therefore it is of the utmost importance to analyse organizations in relation to other organizations and not treat them as single entities.

The influence of technology

It is accepted as commonplace today that the kind of technology used by the organization determines various organizational and structural characteristics. However, this is a relatively new finding, and one which can too easily be taken for granted. In the last decade many writers have stressed the importance of the technology. Of these, the

72

first to realize and systematically investigate this relationship is still the most important in the sense of having made the greatest contribution: Joan Woodward's study of firms in South East Essex in the mid-fifties has done much to demonstrate the influence of technology specifically on industrial organizations. Later work has adapted and refined her findings to include other types of organizations. Woodward's work and the influence of her work can be shown from a later statement by Brown (1960) in looking at the relationship between tasks, technologies, and organization. He says, 'optimum organization must be derived from an analysis of the work to be done and the techniques and resources available to do it.' There is a connection between this statement and the work of earlier theorists of organization, but for the moment, without questioning too closely the relationship between 'optimum' in this context and the conceptions of 'rationality' and 'equilibrium' in the respective theoretical models, there is in this statement an idea which is close to that which underlies the work and findings of Woodward.

Woodward's study arose out of a recognition that most of the work done in this country by sociologists who were interested in industrial problems before about 1953 had been mainly concerned with examining working groups and management-worker relationships. There had been little emphasis on the study of organizational problems.

By breaking away from all conventions in the study of industrial organizations, Woodward was able to look at both the line and staff functions in industry and thereby to look at the total organization, rather than separate aspects of it.

All of the manufacturing firms which came within the catchment area of the South East Essex Technical College were studied. All of the firms with fewer than a hundred

73

employees were discounted from the study since it was assumed that firms of this size were too small to have any meaningful formal organization.

The first survey was of all these firms, merely looking at the formal organization and the operating procedures. The informal operation of these firms was largely ignored. A more detailed study was then carried out on a hundred firms. These firms were divided as follows: thirty-five line organization, two functional organization, fifty-nine line-staff organization, and four unclassified. Briefly, Woodward found differences between these firms, but the differences could not be explained in a 'traditional' manner; for example, differences did not arise because of tradition or personality differences. It was felt necessary to examine technical variables to see how these could account for the differences.

By introducing the variable of technology, Woodward distinguishes three broad categories of market-technology situation: unit and small batch, mass, and process production. There are really two broad categories of market relationship in these three categories, together with the additional constraint of product durability and storability:

a   The customer specifies what he wants and the firm agrees to produce to this specification.

b   The firm produces a standardized product for a mass market, in which the customer is non-specific. This may be differentiated: (i) storage of product is, within limits, not difficult, and this can be used to effect a short-term balance between production and consumption; (ii) storage is extremely difficult or impossible, and the market must take production as it is produced, so that there is less margin which can be used to effect a balance.

With these three types of market situation are associated certain categories of 'hardware' technologies:

a   Unit and small batch methods, involving the general purpose machines or tools.

b   (i) Non-automated or flow methods, involving special purpose machines or tools; and (ii) automated flow production methods, involving the use of special purpose machines or plant which is built into an integrated system.

It is recognized that within any one unit, the market-technology characteristics may vary from section to section, or from function to function. As a first approximation, however, the unit may be characterized in this way.

Within these categories, there is a modal form of organization, and all the firms in the category can be said to cluster around this mode. On the usual measure of success, the more 'successful' units appear to fall close to the mode, the less successful are more distant from the mode. These findings on the form of organization appropriate to these three categories suggest that the 'software' technology (that is, the organization) is also associated with the form taken by the market ends of the organization.

The organizational differences identified were of two types: (i) those which were greater between process and unit than between mass and unit; and (ii) those which were greater beween mass and unit than between process and unit.

Dimensions of organization which follow the first pattern include the span of control of the chief executive, the ratio of indirect to direct labour and of administrative and clerical staff to hourly paid workers, the proportion of graduates engaged on production, the proportion of final cost taken up by labour costs, and the number of levels of authority in the hierarchy.

Dimensions of organization which follow the second pattern include the span of control of the first line supervisor (biggest in mass), the 'flexibility' of the organization, the form of communication as between written (biggest in mass) and oral, the amount of specialization between the functions of management and the separation between the 'brainwork' or administration of production and the actual supervision of production (widest in mass).

Woodward also suggests that these three categories are distinguishable in the basic organizational function which is given most emphasis (and which is therefore likely to wield greatest 'power' within the organization). In unit and small batch, the design/product development function, in mass, the production function, and in process, the marketing function, carried most weight and received most emphasis.

Woodward's work is important from the point of view of analysing organizations because she does indicate certain 'middle-range' propositions. Her findings suggest that there are no 'universal' rules governing the design or the shape of production organizations, except at the level of generalization involved in the bureaucratic and system models. But a number of more 'specific' rules can be recognized as applying to limited sub-categories of production organization, such as those which Woodward identifies. Whilst it must be admitted that these findings are first approximations, they do suggest that the start of any exercise in organization building entails delimitation of the market objectives. From this, on the basis of 'what most often is successful provides the norm or what ought to be', can be derived propositions about the form of organization appropriate to the circumstances and to the ends sought.

Since Woodward's 'pioneering' work on the influence of technology on production organization, many studies have confirmed and elaborated the original statements. In the same vein as Woodward, for example, Harvey (1968) has examined the relationship between organizational characteristics and increasing technical specificity. Harvey showed that as technical specificity increases then the number of organizational sub-units, the number of levels of authority, the ratio of managers and supervisors to total personnel, and the amount of 'programme specification', all increase correspondingly. The classification used by Harvey for production organizations was technically diffuse, technically intermediate, and technically specific.

Having established the linkage between organizational characteristics and degree of technology, Harvey then attempted to relate the organizational characteristics to a series of variables—size, location, environment, form of ownership and control, and general historical factors. There were no significant relationships with any of these variables.

Harvey's classification of organizations according to their degree of technical specificity is similar to Blauner's classification of four types of technology (Blauner, 1964). These types range from 'craft' industries to 'process' industries, providing a continuum of standardization and rationalization. Thus, craft industries display the minimum of standardization and rationalization; 'machine-minding' industries show a fairly high degree of standardization and mechanization; 'assembly-line' industries are highly rationalized and tasks are highly fragmented; and 'process' industries are the most highly mechanized. From this classification of organizations by their technology, Blauner arrives at the same kinds of conclusions as Woodward. Specifically, though, Blauner was more interested in examining relationships which existed between individuals in industrial organizations than in looking at relationships between organizational characteristics. His work does demonstrate, however, that an environmental influence such as the technology can affect social relationships within the organization itself. For example, he makes the point that assembly-line production is more likely to produce an alienative work-force than say a craft industry. The work of Sayles (1958) and Touraine (1955) confirms this.

The influence of technology on other types of organizations can be demonstrated by reference to the hospital organization. In particular the influence on the power structure of the hospital can be examined. It must be recognized that, today, the modern hospital represents an extremely complex and technologically advanced organization, and that this has not always been so. Also, the hospital displays what Goss (1963) calls an advisory bureaucracy. That is, there is a dual authority structure composed essentially of the medical and the administrative structures.

Perrow (1965) makes the point that the technology of the hospital influences the power structure and determines which group possessing authority within the organization will be ascendant. Thus, when the technology is simple, society as a whole dominates the hospital organization; as the technology becomes complex and beyond the comprehension of the layman, it is the medical staff who exercise domination; and the position in the hospital situation today, where there are a great many specialized professional personnel requiring co-ordination for the achievement of the organizational objective, is that the administrator is in the ascendancy.

Parallel to this development in the technology, one can also observe a change in the nature of the goals of the

hospital organization. At the first stage, with society having
control, the basic objective is one of alleviation of pain.
Where the medical structure dominates, there is a great
concern with technical efficiency. At the last stage with
the rise of the administrator, there is increased concern
with the social consequences of illness (Halmos, 1970) as
well as the medical aspects.

Other environmental influences

The study of the Scottish Electronics Industry by Burns and
Stalker (1961) represents, in part, a further attempt to
identify environmental influences upon organizations. The
research was not specifically concerned with conditions
external to the organization. Rather, it was a study of how
management in firms associated with the Scottish Council
could adapt to the challenge of the electronics industry in
Scotland in the mid-fifties. The firms studied were all of
small to medium size, most of them having a fairly successful history. In looking at managerial response to innovation (for example, the establishment of research and de-
development departments in the companies), Burns and
Stalker arrived at two polar types of organization. These
they called mechanistic and organic systems. They found
that these two extreme types could be related to various
conditions external to the organization in question.

Basically, mechanistic systems are appropriate when there
are stable conditions and organic systems are appropriate
to changing conditions. The former system represents a
formal rational type of organization, being characterized,
for example, by strict hierarchic control, vertical interaction, specialized division of labour, and so on. The
organic system is characterized more by lateral communica-

tion, organizational commitment, a more cosmopolitan attitude, and so on.

Burns and Stalker make the point that these two types of system only represent the polar extremes of what can be viewed as a continuum. Most companies would lie somewhere around the middle of this continuum, but it is useful because it enables one to distinguish degrees of mechanistic or organic features in an organization. In this context, Burns and Stalker are important in demonstrating that environmental conditions can have consequences for the organization as a whole.

Summary

Whereas in the last chapter the analysis of organizations was widened by discussing the possibility of studying several types of organizations simultaneously, this chapter broadens the analysis still further. The boundaries of an organization are taken to be problematical and the influence of a series of environmental factors is examined. It is shown that organizations interact with one another and influence each other to varying degrees. Also, technology, in its broadest sense, is discussed as an external influence upon the internal functioning of an organization. The major works in this area are in the field of industrial organizations, but the effect of technology on other types of organizations can be appreciated from the example given of hospitals.

6
Problems in the study of organizations

In any specific discipline or branch of a discipline there are always problems which need to be resolved if that discipline is going to advance. The study of organizations is no exception to this proposition. Problems exist both at a very general level and at a very specific level. These need to be resolved if the study of organizations is to maintain and to increase its status in the social sciences. An analysis of problems in a text of this nature must necessarily be selective and to some extent subjective, but it is hoped that these will indicate that sociologists and other social scientists alike have a long way to go before they can meaningfully talk of a universally applicable theory of organizations.

An industrial bias

One recurring problem which is visible in most texts on organizational analysis is the bias towards the study of industrial organizations to the relative exclusion of other types of organizations. The present text itself is certainly hindered by this bias. The reasons for this are quite simple, the main one being that most research has been carried out in these organizations. Industry has provided a good 'strategic site' for the study of organizations because of its size, complexity, and diversity. One can find industrial organizations varying in size from a handful of people to those employing tens of thousands. Complexity, too, can vary from the most simple 'organization chart' of two hierarchical levels to one with dozens of different levels. Again, diversity is a characteristic of such organizations varying from the publicly-owned undertaking to the strictly privately-owned. These, and other, characteristics of industry have attracted researchers who wanted to study organizations. The result is that this industrial bias inevitably creeps into any general analysis of organizations.

The greater emphasis upon industrial organizations does not mean that other types of organizations have been ignored by theorists and researchers alike. March's authoritative work (1965) examines schools, hospitals, prisons, trade unions, political parties, the civil service, and more. In all of these areas much has been achieved which contributes to our increased understanding.

In this and the next chapter the problems and trends considered will attempt to avoid the general bias of industry. In fact, it will not be necessary to consider any particular type of organization since the problems which exist are common to the study of all types.

One further point which can be said in favour of analysing industrial organizations to the relative exclusion of other types is that the kinds of topics which are examined can be generalized so as to be relevant to other types of organization. For example, the study of industrial organizations as bureaucracies, the nature of the authority structure, of decision-making and problem-solving, types of leadership traits, and so on, are all relevant to the study of other types of organization. It is when specific industrial topics are analysed that the emphasis towards industry is restrictive. For example, an analysis of management-worker relationships tends to be germane to the industrial organization rather than to other types, although there is still some relevance.

From an earlier discussion, it is hypothesized here that the comparative method of analysis in organization will enable the industrial bias to decrease. The comparative method would appear to be the immediate trend for the future, and so the traditional case-study approach will decline in importance.

This discussion on the emphasis on industrial organizations should not be taken to mean that other types of organization have been ignored. In many cases they have been rigorously examined and from these studies great strides have been made in our general understanding of organizations. A few of these areas of analysis can be examined.

Educational organizations and institutions come second in importance to industrial organizations as far as increasing our knowledge is concerned. The methodological approach in studies of educational organizations has been that of an analysis of the roles of organization members. There tend to be very few studies of educational organizations themselves, as studied from the organizational level of analysis. The same comment applies to the analysis of research organizations and military organizations.

Two other major types of organizations, hospitals and prisons, have been studied in some depth and appear to have been much influenced by results from the empirical study of other types of organization. Specific organizational characteristics have been studied in these areas. For example, prisons present a good opportunity to analyse the structural characteristics of goals and organizational conflict. Hospitals, on the other hand, enable the researcher to examine the conflict between the bureaucratic and the professional organization in one setting. Because of an emphasis of this nature in hospital studies, it might be more apt to say that these represent work done in the area of the sociology of professions rather than in the sociology of organizations. This proposition is reinforced by the fact that the role level of analysis has predominated. The study of prisons however does present a greater organizational emphasis.

Another type of organization, the administrative organization, has been under-studied from a sociological point of view because, Mayntz (1964) suggests, the study of administrative structures was established before the study of organizations *per se*. By saying that they have been under-studied sociologically we mean that the traditions of history and political science have been given more emphasis in such analyses. Studies of administrative structures have proved to be useful in the study of organizations in general, particularly when there has been a study of comparative administration.

Organizational sociology has also been concerned with the study of religious organizations, voluntary organizations of all kinds, and others. Despite this any charge that there has been a bias towards the analysis of industrial organizations is a well-founded one, but one which is unlikely to hold for very much longer.

A theory of organization

One of the obvious themes of this book so far has been the fact that the study of organizations does not represent a codified body of theory. In previous chapters the various attempts which have been made at producing a general theory have been discussed. Organizations have been approached by many different types of social scientists—the sociologist, the social psychologist, the economist, the political scientist—and their one aim has been to produce a theory of organization which is empirically relevant and conceptually valid.

In a sense all of the problems analysed here are concerned with the achievement of such a unified theory. Clearly, if the problems which exist in a sociological approach to organizational analysis can be identified and solved, then this must aid the task of unification.

It would be wrong to talk of organizational problems as such; it is necessary to delineate the level of analysis at which particular problems occur. In a previous chapter three levels of analysis were discussed—role, structural, and organizational. For the purposes of this discussion, this schema will not be pursued, but rather the three levels of role, organization, and society will be taken (this follows closely the schema laid down by Mayntz, 1964). It has already been shown that the middle level, that of the organization, is the one which is currently receiving most attention from researchers on organizations, although the level of role analysis is widely used in particular types of organization.

At the lowest level of analysis of the schema under consideration, the emphasis is upon the individual. There is a tendency for research at this level to be more socio-psychologically orientated than sociologically. The emphasis appears to be upon human relations, rather than upon organizational problems. This is not to say that analyses at the level of the role ought to be discounted when considering organizations. Often, studies at this level can provide useful insights into organizational functioning. The main problem arises when researchers suggest that features which are present at the level of the role are automatically

85

features present at the level of the organization. What occurs in fact is a kind of reductionism, summed up in the phrase 'the whole is greater than the sum of the parts'. Most organizational analysts are aware of this problem and attempt to overcome it. To illustrate this point, for example, Blau and Scott (1963) make the distinction between a busload of passengers having nothing in common except the fact that they are bus passengers, and a busload of passengers who belong to a club and are on an outing. In the case of the former, it might be true to say that the whole is not greater than the sum of the parts, but with the latter this proposition is invalid. Similarly with the study of organizations. It is possible to examine the roles of every organization member, but aggregating these roles does not provide an analysis of an organization. Precisely this point is made by Mouzelis (1967) in his analysis of what have here been called the psychological approaches to organizational study, characterized by the work of Simon and March.

Therefore as far as the role level of analysis is concerned, by itself it is not particularly helpful in organizational analysis. It can provide useful guidelines as to the functioning of the larger organization, but the problem of reductionism is always present, thus providing a major drawback.

At the highest level of analysis, that of society, there are major problems which inhibit the growth of a unified organization theory. One such problem is the nature and types of organizations and the way that they impinge upon the wider society. Basically most organizations exhibit features of a bureaucratic system. It has been shown that bureaucracies are characterized by rationalism, and it is suggested that this very rationalism has consequences for society as a whole. Weber himself made this point in his analysis of the growth of Western society. He saw that the bureaucratic structures became identified with society and as such posed the problem of the control that society has over them.

Again, other types of organizations which are not necessarily bureaucratic in nature have been shown to have an influence upon society in general. Voluntary organizations have both a direct and an indirect effect upon society. The quality of this effect differs from that of the large-scale bureaucracies, in that a smaller section of society is affected by them. Trade unions, for example, have a profound effect upon the social structure of any society, but this effect is particularized. Bureaucracies, on the other hand, tend to have a generalized effect associated with the problems of control.

The way in which voluntary organizations or associations have been studied as shown above has led to problems in organizational analysis. By the use of a political and historical orientation these organizations have been treated in a particularized way. Mayntz (1964) makes the point that these voluntary associations and their study have contributed little to the study of organizations because analysis of them has not been treated with the neutrality that would have occurred if the analysts had been organizational sociologists. Important issues are raised by the study of these associations such as the relationship between their values and the values of society, and the degree of independence or autonomy afforded to each.

Methodology

Another issue which poses a problem in organizational analysis is that of the research methodology and quantitative methods. To a certain extent this problem has been raised several times in the discussion here. Very few research methods specific to organizational analysis have arisen, and the trend has been for tools from other areas of sociology to be used in this area. This, of course, need not necessarily pose a problem. However, because organizational analysis does represent a specific branch of sociology, it would have been anticipated that specific research methods would have developed.

A part of the difficulty arises because of the general approach to the study of organizations. Because the emphasis has been upon the case-study method rather than the comparative method, conventional tools of analysis have been sufficient. With a predictable increase in the use of the comparative method a specific organizational methodology might be expected.

All of this, however, is not to say that nothing has been done in organizational analysis to produce or to refine research methods. To give one example of this, the use of 'activity analysis' has been considerable (Dunkerley, 1969). This involves the systematic observation of organizational members by a team of observers such that a fairly complete analysis is obtained of the communication structure, the decision-making structure, and the problem-solving structure in large-scale organizations. Again, sociometric methods have been refined for organizational use, and so on.

Theoretical issues

So far in this examination of the problems in organizational analysis we have specifically discussed the bias towards organizations which are of an industrial nature, the problem of there being no general theory of organization, and the problem of methodology. In addition to these, there are also of course particular theoretical problems. The fact that there is not an integration of the various approaches to the study of organizations is itself a theoretical problem which has already been dealt with at some length.

It would appear that people who now study organizations are no longer concerned whether their approach is sociological, psychological, economic, or otherwise. For example, the study of organizations by Pugh and Hickson referred to earlier was carried out by a multidisciplinary team. Many researchers into organizations would not see themselves as having allegiance to any particular discipline. If the trend is towards a multidisciplinary approach to organizations, then it might reasonably be assumed that something new in the way of a theory of organizations might emerge.

From a theoretical point of view part of the problem in the study of organizations has been that up until comparatively recently the emphasis in research has been upon testing specific propositions and, furthermore, that these propositions have been germane to one specific type of organization. It might be hypothesized that in the immediate future investigations will be carried out which go further than the mere testing of specific propositions and that this will be done on a comparative level.

Summary

In discussing the problems associated with the analysis of organizations it has by now become clear that the overriding problem is that of the search for a general theory which is universally applicable. Of course, other problems are derived from this central issue and thus are necessarily of less significance. Some writers question the usefulness of attempting to arrive at a general integrated theory. Their argument is that as the theory becomes more generally applicable, then the propositions and the conceptual framework of which the theory is composed must themselves become more general in nature. The point made is that a theory composed of very generalized propositions is automatically devalued as a theory.

As is made clear in the following chapter, the present writer is committed to the idea that a unified theory of organization is both possible to achieve, and furthermore, would aid the future development of studies of organizations. The charge of the generality of the propositions is answered by the fact that this is only likely to occur if only one discipline contributes to the formulation of such a generalized theory. By using a multidisciplinary approach to the study of organizations more specific propositions are possible, but ones which are nevertheless applicable to all types of organizations.

7
Summary and future trends

The examination here of some of the major current trends and thought in the study of organizations has suggested several things. It is clear that organizations constitute a major part of any urban society and as such have an influence upon that society. From this perspective, organizations can be studied sociologically. Again, because of the extensiveness of organizations, most individuals are at some time or another organization members. Thus, organizations in some way or other do influence and affect the lives of the individuals of which society is composed.

If a central theme can be delineated from this book, it is that at the present time there is no one theory of organization. Such a theory is considered imperative for two main reasons. Firstly, by having an integrated theory, research in this area of sociology could advance from the 'diagnostic' level of analysis to the 'prescriptive' level, and secondly the problems associated with the interaction of organizations and the 'societal level' could be more systematically investigated.

It has been shown that organizations have been studied by researchers from varying disciplines and that as yet they have not produced a general theory. The bias here has been to examine those sociological theories, although the influence of, say, social psychology and political science has been recognized. By simply taking the sociological approach, it has become clear that research procedures have improved greatly and that the conception of the organization has broadened to include the external environment and not simply to emphasize the internal structure of the organization.

A convergence of approaches is visible in the study of organizations. The use of middle-range theories of the kind that Woodward and Etzioni have proposed has done much to bring this about. As a result of research in the last fifteen years Gouldner's view of the state of organizational analysis being a choice between the formal and the natural system model would no longer be true today. The simple dichotomous position has been eroded by the use of middle-range theories. A realistic prediction concerning future trends would be an increased input of resources measuring variables of the middle range.

In the final analysis it has to be recognized that sociology has attempted to examine the problems which the ubiquity of organizations in society has produced. The stage has been reached where a specific discipline has emerged for the study of such organizations and, as Silverman rightly points out, the 'discipline' of 'formal organizations' is 'a new animal with a hungry appetite' (Silverman, 1968, p.221). Silverman proposes a social action model for the examination of these formal organizations, and that such a model should come within the framework of industrial sociology (Silverman, 1970).

As a future trend it is possible that a social action approach to organizations may provide some of the required answers in the analysis of organization but it would appear to be a retrogressive step to place the study of organizations back in industrial sociology when it is only just beginning to emerge from that influence and to widen its boundaries.

The approach to organizational analysis used in this work has been implicitly historical. It is clear from this that the study of organizations has passed through roughly the same stage of development as other branches of sociology. In the first place, the early thinkers on organizations examined them at a macroscopic level, then the emphasis shifted such that the focus was upon the individual within the organization. The next stage was for the structural features of the organization to be studied and, lastly, the organization was examined in relation to the external environment. The emerging trend appears to be that of comparative analysis. If there is some kind of a 'natural law' for the development of specific branches of sociology, then the study of organizations has reached the stage where it is necessary for other disciplines to be involved and for the whole frame of reference to be broadened.

As the last chapter has demonstrated, there are a great many problems inherent in the study of organizations, but these stem basically from the inability of the 'discipline' to achieve integration. This is not to say that if a general theory of organization is produced in the future all problems of organizational analysis will disappear, for as one problem is solved other problems emerge. What can be said is that the major contemporary stumbling-block for the development of organizational analysis will have been removed.

Suggestions for further reading

There is considerable literature in the area of organizational analysis, but the reading suggested here aims at the more recent texts. Each of them contains good review material and then progresses towards a more specific theme. The combination of these with the references used in the main bibliography should provide the reader with a comprehensive guide to the important literature in this area.

ALBROW, M. C. (1970), *Bureaucracy*, London, Pall Mall.
BURNS, T. (1969), *Industrial Man*, Harmondsworth, Penguin Books.
ETZIONI, A. (1969), *Readings on Modern Organizations*, Englewood Cliffs, N.J., Prentice-Hall.
FOX, A. (1971), *A Sociology of Work in Industry*, London, Collier-Macmillan.
GRUSKY, O. and MILLER, G. A. (1970), *The Sociology of Organisations*, New York, Free Press.
MOUZELIS, N. (1967), *Organization and Bureaucracy*, London, Routledge & Kegan Paul.
PERROW, C. (1970), *Organisational Analysis*, London, Tavistock Publications.
SILVERMAN, D. (1970), *The Theory of Organisations*, London, Heinemann.

Bibliography

AARONOVITCH, S. (1955), *Monopoly: A Study of British Monopoly Capitalism*, London, Lawrence & Wishart.

BARNARD, C. I. (1938), *The Functions of the Executive*, Harvard University Press.

BERLE, A. A. and MEANS, G. C. (1933), *The Modern Corporation and Private Property*, New York, Macmillan.

BLAU, P. M. (1955), *The Dynamics of Bureaucracy*, Cambridge University Press.

BLAU, P. M. (1956), *Bureaucracy In Modern Society*, New York, Random House.

BLAU, P. M. (1965), 'The Comparative Study of Organizations', *Industrial and Labor Relations Review*, Vol. 18, pp. 323-38.

BLAU, P. M. and SCOTT, W. G. (1963), *Formal Organizations: A Comparative Approach*, London, Routledge & Kegan Paul.

BLAUNER, R. (1964), *Alienation and Freedom*, Chicago University Press.

BOTTOMORE, T. B. and RUBEL, M. (eds) (1956), *Karl Marx, Selected Writings in Sociology and Social Philosophy*, London, C. A. Watts.

BROWN, W. (1960), *Exploration in Management*, London, Heinemann.

BIBLIOGRAPHY

BURNS, T. and STALKER, G. M. (1961), *The Management of Innovation*, London, Tavistock Publications.

CYERT, R. M. and MARCH, J. G. (1963), *A Behavioral Theory of the Firm*, New York, Free Press.

DUNKERLEY, D. (1969), *Techniques of Analysis of Executive Behaviour*, Cardiff, University of Wales.

ETZIONI, A. (1961), *A Comparative Analysis of Complex Organizations*, London, Collier-Macmillan.

ETZIONI, A. (ed.) (1961), *A Sociological Reader on Complex Organizations*, New York, Holt, Rinehart, & Winston.

FLORENCE, P. S. (1964), *Economics and Sociology of Industry*, London, Watts.

GERTH, H. H. and MILLS, C. W. (1948), *From Max Weber: Essays in Sociology*, London, Routledge & Kegan Paul.

GOSS, M. E. W. (1963), 'Patterns of Bureaucracy among Hospital Staff Physicians', in Friedson, M. E. (ed.), *The Hospital in Modern Society*, New York, Free Press, pp. 170-94.

GOULDNER, A. W. (1955), *Patterns of Industrial Bureaucracy*, London, Routledge & Kegan Paul.

GOULDNER, A. W. (1959), 'Organizational Analysis', in Merton, R. K. Broom, L., and Cottrell, L. S. (eds), *Sociology Today*, London, Mayflower.

HALMOS, P. (1970), *The Personal Service Society*, London, Constable.

HANIKA, F. de P. (1965), *New Thinking In Management*, London, Hutchinson.

HARVEY, E. (1968), 'Technology and the Structure of Organisations', *American Sociological Review*, 33, pp.247-59.

HENDERSON, L. J. (1936), *Pareto's General Sociology*, Harvard University Press.

HOMANS, G. C. (1951), *The Human Group*, London, Routledge & Kegan Paul.

HOMANS, G. C. (1961), *Social Behavior: Its Elementary Forms*, New York, Harcourt, Brace, & World.

HOMANS, G. C. (1962), *Sentiments and Activities: Essays in Social Science*, London, Routledge & Kegan Paul.

JAQUES, E. (1961), *Equitable Payment*, London, Heinemann.

LANDSBERGER, H. A. (1958), *Hawthorne Revisited*, Cornell University Press.

LEWIN, K. (1953), *Field Theory in Social Science*, New York, Harper.

LUPTON, T. (1963), *On the Shop Floor*, London, Pergamon.

MARCH, J. G. (ed.) (1965), *Handbook of Organizations*, New York, Rand McNally.

MARCH, J. G. and SIMON, H. A. (1958), *Organizations*, New York, Wiley.

MAYNTZ, R. (1964), 'The Study of Organizations', *Current Sociology*, Vol. 13, pp.94-119.

MERTON, R. K. (1949), *Social Theory and Social Structure*, Chicago, Free Press.

MICHELS, R. (1949), *Political Parties*, Chicago, Free Press.

MILLER, D. C. and FORM, W. H. (1964), *Industrial Sociology*, New York, Harper Bros.

MOUZELIS, N. (1967), *Organization and Bureacracy*, London, Routledge & Kegan Paul.

PARKER, S. R., BROWN, R. K., CHILD, J., and SMITH, M. A. (1967), *The Sociology of Industry*, London, Allen & Unwin.

PARSONS, T. (1951), *The Social System*, Chicago, Free Press.

PARSONS, T. (1956), 'Suggestions for a Sociological Approach to the Theory of Organizations', *Administrative Science Quarterly*, Vol. 1, pp.63-85, 224-39.

PARSONS, T. (1960), *Structure and Process in Modern Societies*, Chicago, Free Press.

PERROW, C. (1961), 'The Analysis of Goals in Complex Organizations', *American Sociological Review*, Vol. 26, pp.854-67.

PERROW, C. (1965), 'Hospitals: Technology, Structure and

Goals', in March, J. G., *Handbook of Organizations*, New York, Rand McNally, pp.910-71.

PERROW, C. (1967), 'A Framework for the Comparative Analysis of Organisations', *American Sociological Review*, pp.194-208.

PUGH, D. A., HICKSON, D. J. and HININGS, C. R. (1969), 'An Empirical Taxonomy of Structures of Work Organizations', *Administrative Science Quarterly*, Vol. 14, pp.115-26.

ROETHLISBERGER, F. J. and DICKSON, W. J. (1961), *Management and the Worker*, Harvard University Press.

SAYLES, L. R. (1958), *Behavior of Industrial Work Groups*, New York, Wiley.

SCOTT, W. R. (1964), 'The Theory of Organisations', in Faris, E. (ed.), *Handbook of Modern Sociology*, New York, Rand McNally, pp.485-529.

SELZNICK, P. (1948), 'Foundations of the Theory of Organizations', *American Sociological Review*, Vol. 13, pp.23-35.

SHEPPARD, H. L. (1949), 'The Treatment of Unionism in "Managerial Sociology"', *American Sociological Review*, Vol. 14, pp.310-13.

SHEPPARD, H. L. (1954), 'Approaches to Conflict in American Industrial Sociology', *British Journal of Sociology*, Vol. 5, pp.324-41.

SILVERMAN, D. (1968), 'Formal Organisations or Industrial Sociology?', *Sociology*, Vol. 2, pp.221-38.

SIMON, H. A. (1957), *Administrative Behaviour*, London, Collier-Macmillan.

SORENSON, R. C. (1951), 'The Concept of Conflict in Industrial Sociology', *Social Forces*, pp.263-7.

THOMPSON, J. D. and MCEWEN, W. J. (1958), 'Organizational Goals and Environment', *American Sociological Review*, Vol. 23, pp.23-31.

TOURAINE, A. (1955), *L'Evolution du travail ouvrier aux*

usines Renault, Paris, Centre National de la Recherche Scientifique.

UDY, S. H. (1957), 'Bureaucracy and Rationality in Weber's Organization Theory', *American Sociological Review*, Vol. 22, pp.791-5.

UDY, S. H. (1965), 'The Comparative Analysis of Organisations', in March, J. G. (1965), *Handbook of Organizations*, New York, Rand McNally, pp.678-709.

WEBER, M. (1957), *The Theory of Social and Economic Organizations*, London, Collier-Macmillan.

WHITE, R., and LIPPITT, R. (1953), 'Leader Behaviour and Member Reaction in Three "Social Climates"', in Cartwright, D. and Zander, A. (eds), *Group Dynamics*, London, Tavistock, pp.585-611.

WOODWARD, J. (1958), *Management and Technology*, London, H.M.S.O.

WOODWARD, J. (1965), *Industrial Organization, Theory and Practice*, London, Oxford University Press.